Survey Instrument to Assess the Prevalence of Hazing and Bullying in the Active-Duty U.S. Military

MIRIAM MATTHEWS, COREEN FARRIS, ANDREW R. MORRAL,
TERRY L. SCHELL, KIRSTEN M. KELLER

Prepared for Office of Secretary of Defense
Approved for public release; distribution unlimited

RAND NATIONAL DEFENSE RESEARCH INSTITUTE

For more information on this publication, visit **www.rand.org/t/RRA1246-1**.

Published by the RAND Corporation, Santa Monica, Calif.

Library of Congress Cataloging-in-Publication Data is available for this publication.
ISBN: 978-1-9774-0781-8

Cover: U.S. Army photo by Matthew Moeller.

About This Research Report

The U.S. Department of Defense (DoD) sought to implement a new measurement of hazing and bullying in the armed forces. The new measurement needed to align with military definitions and policy, and it needed to apply across the military services. This report describes the development and design of a survey instrument to help DoD estimate the number of active-duty service members who experience hazing and bullying. This report should be of interest to those who wish to better understand measurement of hazing and bullying, including academic researchers, and those responsible for understanding and addressing hazing and bullying in the military, including equal opportunity professionals.

The research reported here was completed in June 2021 and underwent security review with the sponsor and the Defense Office of Prepublication and Security Review before public release.

RAND National Security Research Division

This research was sponsored by the Office of the Secretary of Defense and conducted within the Forces and Resources Policy Center of the RAND National Security Research Division, which operates the National Defense Research Institute, a federally funded research and development center sponsored by the Office of the Secretary of Defense, the Joint Staff, the Unified Combatant Commands, the Navy, the Marine Corps, the defense agencies, and the defense intelligence enterprise.

For more information on the Forces and Resources Policy Center, see www.rand.org/nsrd/ndri/centers/frp or contact the director (contact information is provided on the webpage).

Acknowledgments

We wish to thank the individuals at the Office of People Analytics who provided input on this project, including Samantha Daniel, Carol Newell, and Paul Rosenfeld. We would also like to thank those in the former Office of Diversity Management and Equal Opportunity who supported, provided information to, and participated in discussions with us, including Shirley Raguindin and Charmane Johnson. In addition, we thank the multiple service members who reviewed and commented on the survey. We also thank the following subject-matter experts—Elizabeth Allan, Joel Neuman, Jennifer Waldron, and David Yamada—for their contributions, thoughtful comments, and suggestions regarding the survey; and we thank Mary Madden for her thoughtful review of this report. We thank our RAND colleagues Laura Miller, Lisa Jaycox, and Kim Hall for their comments on previous survey drafts, and we thank Barbara Bicksler for her editorial review and comments.

Contents

Tables

Summary

In 2016, the Office of People Analytics (OPA) and the Office of Diversity Management and Equal Opportunity (ODMEO) asked the RAND Corporation to develop a survey instrument to measure the incidence of hazing and bullying in the active-duty U.S. military.[1] To assess the prevalence of these behaviors, the instrument needed to align with the developing definitions of hazing and bullying, originally described in the 2015 U.S. Department of Defense (DoD) memorandum on these behaviors (Work, 2015). In addition, the instrument was to be included within a larger DoD-conducted survey effort, such as the Workplace and Equal Opportunity (WEO) surveys or the Status of Forces surveys (Defense Manpower Data Center, 2016).[2] These surveys use multiple survey items to address a diversity of topics, so, to reduce the possibility of survey fatigue, DoD asked RAND to use a limited number of survey items (approximately ten) to assess service member experiences of hazing and bullying behaviors. In April 2017, RAND researchers delivered a brief survey instrument designed to collect the information necessary to estimate the percentage of service members who had experienced hazing and bullying in the past year. After edits by the sponsor, it was fielded as part of the 2017 WEO survey. Later, in February 2018, DoD finalized DoD Instruction (DoDI) 1020.03, *Harassment Prevention and Response in the Armed Forces*, which contained new definitions of hazing and bullying.

The purpose of this report is to describe the original cognitive testing of the fielded instrument and recommended revisions to improve the instrument without precluding trend analysis between the original fielding and subsequent fieldings. For context, the report also offers a short description of the development and design of the survey instrument and describes how the wording in the proposed items compares with the final wording used in DoDI 1020.03.

---

1 As of 2018, policy and practices to prevent and respond to hazing and bullying are now overseen by the Office of Diversity, Equity, and Inclusion.

2 DoD subsequently included a version of the instrument in the WEO survey effort that was administered during the fall of 2017.

Study Analytic Approach

To develop this instrument, RAND researchers reviewed current and past metrics that have been used by DoD, academic, and private sectors to measure the prevalence of hazing and bullying. We also assembled a team of recognized experts in survey design, hazing, and bullying to assist with instrument development and review. We then developed a survey metric that could be used to estimate the percentage of active-duty service members who may have experienced hazing and bullying in the past year, as defined in military policy. We coordinated with experts from academia, ODMEO, DoD's Office of General Counsel, and sponsor-identified stakeholders, as needed, to revise and vet the draft measure. After development of a draft survey instrument, we conducted cognitive interviews with a small but diverse sample of active-duty service members to help identify unclear instructions or item wording that could produce errors in survey measurement.[3]

Final Instrument Design

In an initial review of the hazing and bullying literature, incorporating publications from 1990 to 2017, we found that no existing measures were a precise fit to the new DoD definitions. Therefore, we constructed new, military-specific measures of the percentage of active-duty service members who experience hazing and bullying each year that align with the newly developed definitions. In developing the new measures, the research team drew on the previous measures reviewed and expert feedback obtained to help refine the initial draft measure provided to DoD. A later review of literature published between 2017 and 2021 found that the RAND-developed instrument continued to most closely align with DoD definitions of hazing and bullying, relative to other publicly available measures.

As mentioned previously, DoD intended to use the RAND-developed instrument as part of the 2017 WEO or Status of Forces surveys and indeed

---

[3] Cognitive interviewing is a widely used method in survey development that allows researchers to examine how participants interpret survey instructions, items, and response options (Willis, 2005).

did incorporate a version of the instrument into the 2017 WEO survey. Because of the time constraints imposed by the survey deadlines, RAND researchers were unable to conduct cognitive interviews until after an initial draft of the instrument was provided to DoD. DoD revised the instrument that RAND had provided, changing the design structure and adding two final questions. Rather than including an initial screening item addressing a class of harm and immediately presenting two follow-up items to those who indicated that they had experienced the referenced class of harm, the revised instrument first addresses all broad classes of harm or risks of harm. Then, follow-up items address characteristics of these experiences. The structure was revised with the goal of facilitating ease of programming. A hard copy of this revised version subsequently was used during cognitive interviews.

Discussions during the cognitive interviews prompted the RAND team to make some revisions to survey items and also suggested other modifications to the survey that may be warranted.

RAND researchers modified several items in the instrument to improve clarity. For example, text was modified to clarify that the questions were applicable to both service members and civilians who worked for the military and to remove and replace terminology that raised questions among interview participants.

Participants in the cognitive interviews raised concerns about the new questions added by DoD. Participants were doubtful that the open-ended question could be meaningfully answered without disclosing personally identifying information and suggested that many respondents would likely skip the question. Thus, the RAND research team recommends that DoD consider removing the open-ended question from the final survey. Interviewees also found the final question on cyberbullying awkward, given that some of the behaviors included in the instrument can only occur in person. The RAND team thus also recommends that some adjustment be made to this question if it is retained so that it is not asked of respondents who experienced only behaviors that cannot occur online (see Chapter Four).

Participants found the DoD-revised survey design cumbersome. Some indicated a preference for follow-up questions to appear immediately after a respondent indicated that he or she had experienced a particular negative behavior—the approach used by the RAND team in its initial design.

The more streamlined design strategy initially used by the RAND research team was approved by survey development experts internal and external to RAND as a survey design strategy that reduces the cognitive load of respondents and increases the ease with which they can respond to items. Thus, the DoD-revised survey could be increasing the cognitive load on respondents. Nevertheless, the final instrument provided to OPA is based on the DoD-revised format wherein participants first address whether they experienced broad classes of harm or risks of harm and then revisit the same list of harmful behaviors two additional times to address characteristics of these experiences. We recommend that DoD consider using the original format suggested by the RAND research team. However, we include the final instrument because it addresses the survey programming requirements of DoD.

Abbreviations

DoD	U.S. Department of Defense
DoDI	Department of Defense Instruction
GAO	U.S. General Accounting Office
GWHQ	Generalized Workplace Harassment Questionnaire
HABS-CS	Hospital Aggressive Behaviour Scale–version Co-workers-Superiors
LIPT	Leymann Inventory of Psychological Terrorization
NAQ	Negative Acts Questionnaire
NAQ-R	Negative Acts Questionnaire—Revised
ODMEO	Office of Diversity Management and Equal Opportunity
OPA	Office of People Analytics
PII	personally identifiable information
SERE	survival, evasion, resistance, and escape
WCM	Workplace Cyberbullying Measure
WEO	Workplace and Equal Opportunity
WEOA	Workplace and Equal Opportunity Survey of Active Duty
WHS	Work Harassment Scale

CHAPTER ONE

Introduction

The U.S. Department of Defense (DoD) is committed to eliminating hazing and bullying among military service members and civilian employees. DoD reiterated this commitment in a 2015 memorandum on hazing and bullying prevention and response (Work, 2015) and through the development and implementation of Department of Defense Instruction (DoDI) 1020.03, *Harassment Prevention and Response in the Armed Forces* (Office of the Under Secretary of Defense for Personnel and Readiness, 2018). These documents improve on a previous 1997 DoD policy memorandum by providing an updated definition of hazing; introducing a definition of bullying; and delivering additional guidance on training, education, tracking, and reporting of these prohibited behaviors (Cohen, 1997; Office of Diversity Management and Equal Opportunity [ODMEO], 2017).

An estimate of the annual prevalence of hazing and bullying in the military services would provide an important baseline by which to judge the effectiveness of the prevention and response efforts outlined in DoDI 1020.03. However, existing survey efforts by DoD do not provide an estimate that aligns with the new DoD definitions of hazing and bullying. Although the Workplace and Equal Opportunity (WEO) surveys and the Service Academy Gender Relations survey collect information on hazing and bullying, the behaviors assessed within these instruments have been limited to those motivated by the race or gender of the victim (e.g., have military or civilian personnel "hazed you [for example, have you experienced forced behaviors that were cruel, abusive, oppressive, or harmful] because of your race/ethnicity?"; Defense Manpower Data Center, 2014; Office of People Analytics [OPA], 2017). In addition, following the updated DoD guidance regarding hazing and bullying, DoD needed a replacement survey instrument that better aligned with new policy and definitions and that could be applied across the military services. As such, even with removal of reference to race/ethnicity or gender from the previous WEO survey items, the example behaviors described within the items did not align with new policy and definitions.

In 2016, OPA and ODMEO asked the RAND Corporation to develop a new survey instrument to measure incidents of hazing and bullying in the active-duty U.S. military. To assess the prevalence of victimization, the instrument needed to align with the developing definitions of hazing and bullying, originally described in the 2015 DoD memorandum on these behaviors (Work, 2015). In addition, the survey instrument was slated for inclusion within either the WEO or the Status of Forces survey (Defense Manpower Data Center, 2016). These surveys use multiple survey items to address a diversity of topics, so, to reduce the possibility of survey fatigue, DoD asked RAND to use a limited number of survey items (approximately ten) to assess service member experiences of hazing and bullying behaviors. In April 2017, RAND researchers delivered a brief survey instrument designed to collect the information necessary to estimate the percentage of service members who had experienced hazing and bullying in the past year. After edits by the sponsor, it was fielded as part of the 2017 WEO. Later, in February 2018, DoDI 1020.03, which contained the DoD's official definitions of hazing and bullying, was finalized and published.

The primary purpose of this report is to describe cognitive testing of the fielded instrument and recommended revisions to improve the instrument without precluding trend analysis between the original fielding and subsequent fieldings. For context, the report also offers a short description of the development process and design of the survey instrument and describes how the wording in the proposed items compares with that of the final wording used in DoDI 1020.03.

Analytic Approach

To develop an instrument to assess the prevalence of hazing and bullying in the active-duty U.S. military, the RAND team completed the following tasks:

- reviewed current and past survey measures that have been used by DoD, academia, and the private sector to measure the prevalence of hazing and bullying

- assembled a team of recognized experts in survey design, hazing, and bullying to advise in the development of a new survey measure
- developed a draft survey measure to estimate the percentage of active-duty service members who may have experienced (1) hazing and (2) bullying in the past year, as defined in military policy
- solicited expert feedback and pretesting to vet the draft instrument and revise as appropriate
- requested feedback from the external expert team
- coordinated with ODMEO, DoD's Office of General Counsel, and sponsor-identified stakeholders, as needed, to vet the draft measure
- after incorporating feedback from expert review, conducted cognitive pretesting with a small but diverse sample of the individuals.

Organization of the Report

The remaining chapters in this report describe the survey development process. Chapter Two provides an overview of the development of the initial draft measure. Chapter Three describes results of and subsequent survey revisions made in response to cognitive interviews, Chapter Four provides the final instrument design after expert review and pretesting (cognitive interviews), and Chapter Five provides a brief conclusion. Appendix A describes the RAND team's review of previous hazing and bullying measures. The report also documents two other versions of the instrument that existed before completion of the final design. Appendix B contains the survey instrument that the RAND research team recommends DoD consider for inclusion in the WEO. Appendix C includes the OPA-revised survey instrument that was fielded in the 2017 WEO and the RAND team's comments on the included changes.

CHAPTER TWO

Initial Development of Draft Hazing and Bullying Measures

As a basis for developing a survey instrument that would be used to estimate the prevalence of hazing and bullying among the U.S. military's active component, the RAND team turned to the official definitions of these terms as stated in DoD instruction. At the time of survey development, RAND used draft language that was being considered for inclusion in DoDI 1020.03, and after instrument development and fielding, the language was finalized.[1] In Table 2.1, we provide the draft language used for instrument development and, for comparison, we also include the final language. In the first two columns, we highlight differences between the draft and final definitions in red, and in the final column, we compare the differences between the two definitions. As seen in Table 2.1, the differences between the draft definitions used to develop the survey instrument and the final definitions published by DoD are minimal.

Comparing key differences between the two types of misconduct, hazing, unlike bullying, requires that behavior be conducted as part of initiation into, or continued membership in, an organization. Bullying, unlike hazing, requires intent to harm. This chapter provides an overview of the specific steps we took to develop a draft hazing and bullying survey instrument to estimate the percentage of active-duty service members who may

[1] DoDI 1020.ef contained draft language to be considered for inclusion in DoD 1020.03, which was issued in February 2018, after creation of the DoD measures of hazing and bullying. The definitions of *hazing* and *bullying* contained in DoDI 1020.03 are almost identical to those that had been listed in DoD 1020.ef, with only minor wording differences.

TABLE 2.1

Department of Defense Definition of Hazing and Bullying

Hazing		
Draft Policy 1020.ef	**Final Policy 1020.03**	**Comparison**
Hazing is any conduct through which a military member or members or a Department of Defense civilian employee or employees, without a proper military or other governmental purpose but with a nexus to military service or Department of Defense civilian employment, physically or psychologically injure or create a risk of physical or psychological injury to one or more military members, Department of Defense civilians, or any other persons for the purpose of: initiation into, admission into, affiliation with, change in status or position within, or as a condition for continued membership in any military or Department of Defense civilian organization. Hazing includes, but is not limited to, the following when performed without a proper military or other governmental purpose: any form of initiation or congratulatory act that involves physically striking another in any manner or threatening to do the same; pressing any object into another person's skin, regardless of whether it pierces the skin, such as "pinning" or "tacking on" of rank insignia, aviator wings, jump wings, diver insignia, badges, medals, or any other object; oral or written berating of another for the purpose of belittling or humiliating; encouraging another to engage in illegal, harmful, demeaning or dangerous acts; playing	HAZING. A form of harassment that includes conduct through which Service members or DoD employees, without a proper military or other governmental purpose but with a nexus to military Service, physically or psychologically injures or creates a risk of physical or psychological injury to Service members for the purpose of: initiation into, admission into, affiliation with, change in status or position within, or a condition for continued membership in any military or DoD civilian organization. Hazing can be conducted through the use of electronic devices or communications, and by other means including social media, as well as in person. a. Hazing is evaluated by a reasonable person standard and includes, but is not limited to, the following when performed without a proper military or other governmental purpose: 1. Any form of initiation or congratulatory act that involves physically striking another person in any manner or threatening to do the same; 2. Pressing any object into another person's skin, regardless of whether it pierces the skin, such as "pinning" or "tacking on" of rank insignia, aviator wings, jump wings, diver insignia, badges, medals, or any other object; 3. Oral or written berating of another person with the purpose of belittling or humiliating; 4. Encouraging another person to engage in illegal, harmful, demeaning or dangerous acts; 5. Playing abusive or malicious tricks;	In the draft policy, neither hazing nor bullying was explicitly described as a form of harassment. The final policy, however, describes both as a form of harassment. The final policy removes explicit reference to civilians from the hazing definition that had been listed in the draft policy—addressing DoD employees, more broadly—and references Service members, rather than military members. DoD employees are not defined elsewhere in the final policy. Unlike the draft policy's, the final policy's hazing definition does not reference physical or psychological injury to "Department of Defense civilians, or any other persons." The focus in the final policy definition is only on injury to Service members. Unlike the draft policy's, the final policy's hazing definition includes the reasonable person standard (see point (a) of the final policy). Unlike the draft policy's, the final policy's hazing definition explicitly references conducting acts against "another person," and includes mention of a "person" in the earlier examples. Points (b), (c), and (d) in the final policy's hazing definition are somewhat

Table 2.1—Continued

Hazing		
Draft Policy 1020.ef	**Final Policy 1020.03**	**Comparison**
abusive or malicious tricks; branding, handcuffing, duct taping, tattooing, shaving, greasing, or painting; subjecting to excessive or abusive use of water; and the forced consumption of food, alcohol, drugs, or any other substance. Hazing can be conducted through the use of electronic devices or communications, and by other means, as well as in person.	6. Branding, handcuffing, duct taping, tattooing, shaving, greasing, or painting another person; 7. Subjecting another person to excessive or abusive use of water; 8. Forcing another person to consume food, alcohol, drugs, or any other substance; and 9. Soliciting, coercing, or knowingly permitting another person to solicit or coerce acts of hazing. b. Hazing does not include properly directed command or organizational activities that serve a proper military or other governmental purpose, or the requisite training activities required to prepare for such activities (e.g., administrative corrective measures, extra military instruction, or command-authorized physical training). c. Service members may be responsible for an act of hazing even if there was actual or implied consent from the victim and regardless of the grade or rank, status, or Service of the victim. d. Hazing is prohibited in all circumstances and environments including off-duty or "unofficial" unit functions and settings.	new text. Point (b) is also captured in point (a) of the final policy. Point (c) was previously only listed at the end of the bullying definition in the draft policy. It is now also included in the hazing definition. In addition, it previously included mention of DoD civilians.
Bullying		
Bullying is an act of aggression by a military member or members, or Department of Defense civilian employee or employees, with a nexus to military service or Department of Defense civilian employment, with the intent of harming a military member, Department of	BULLYING. A form of harassment that includes acts of aggression by Service members or DoD civilian employees, with a nexus to military service, with the intent of harming a Service member either physically or psychologically, without a proper military or other governmental purpose. Bullying may involve the singling out of	In the draft policy, neither hazing nor bullying were explicitly described as a form of harassment. The final policy, however, describes both as a form of harassment. The final policy removes explicit reference to harm to "Department of Defense

Table 2.1—Continued

Bullying		
Draft Policy 1020.ef	**Final Policy 1020.03**	**Comparison**
Defense civilian, or any other persons, either physically or psychologically, without a proper military or other governmental purpose. Bullying may involve the singling out of an individual from his or her co-workers, or unit, for ridicule because he or she is considered different or weak. It often involves an imbalance of power between the aggressor and the victim. Bullying includes, but is not limited to, the following when performed without a proper military or other governmental purpose: physically striking another in any manner or threatening to do the same; intimidating; teasing; taunting; oral or written berating of another for the purpose of belittling or humiliating; encouraging another to engage in illegal, harmful, demeaning, or dangerous acts; playing abusive or malicious tricks; branding, handcuffing, duct taping, tattooing, shaving, greasing, or painting; subjecting to excessive or abusive use of water; the forced consumption of food, alcohol, drugs, or any other substance; and degrading or damaging the person or his or her property or reputation. Bullying can be conducted through the use of electronic devices or communications, and by other means, as well as in person. Soliciting, coercing, or knowingly permitting another person to solicit or coerce acts of hazing or bullying may be considered acts of	an individual from his or her coworkers, or unit, for ridicule because he or she is considered different or weak. It often involves an imbalance of power between the aggressor and the victim. Bullying can be conducted through the use of electronic devices or communications, and by other means including social media, as well as in person. a. Bullying is evaluated by a reasonable person standard and includes, but is not limited to the following when performed without a proper military or other governmental purpose: 1. Physically striking another person in any manner or threatening to do the same; 2. Intimidating, teasing, or taunting another person; 3. Oral or written berating of another person with the purpose of belittling or humiliating; 4. Encouraging another person to engage in illegal, harmful, demeaning or dangerous acts; 5. Playing abusive or malicious tricks; 6. Branding, handcuffing, duct taping, tattooing, shaving, greasing, or painting another person; 7. Subjecting another person to excessive or abusive use of water; 8. Forcing another person to consume food, alcohol, drugs, or any other substance; 9. Degrading or damaging another's property or reputation; and 10. Soliciting, coercing, or knowingly permitting another person to solicit or coerce acts of bullying.	civilians, or any other persons" from the bullying definition listed in the draft policy. The final policy's bullying definition references Service members, rather than the draft policy definition's reference to military members. Unlike the draft policy's, the final policy's bullying definition includes the reasonable person standard (see point (a) of the final policy). Unlike the draft policy's, the final policy's bullying definition explicitly references conducting acts against "another person," and includes mention of a "person" in the earlier examples. Points (b), (c), and (d) in the final policy definition are somewhat new text. Point (b) is also captured in point (a) of the final policy. Point (c) was previously only listed at the end of the bullying definition in the draft policy. In addition, it previously included mention to DoD civilians.

Table 2.1—Continued

Bullying		
Draft Policy 1020.ef	**Final Policy 1020.03**	**Comparison**
hazing or bullying. A military member or Department of Defense civilian employee may still be responsible for or bullying, even if there was actual or implied consent from the victim and regardless of the grade/rank, status or Service or organization of the victim.	b. Bullying does not include properly directed command or organizational activities that serve a proper military or other governmental purpose, or the requisite training activities required to prepare for such activities (e.g., command-authorized physical training). c. Service members may be responsible for an act of bullying even if there was actual or implied consent from the victim and regardless of the grade or rank, status, or Service of the victim. d. Bullying is prohibited in all circumstances and environments, including off-duty or "unofficial" unit functions and settings.	

have experienced hazing and bullying in the past year, as defined in the foregoing military policy. Although other military-specific measures of bullying and hazing have been developed for specific environments (e.g., basic and technical training; Keller et al., 2015; Miller et al., 2019), the goal of this measure was to create a DoD measure that was aligned with policy definitions and applicable to all services. As described in more detail later in this chapter, this goal included addressing the categories of misconduct described within the definitions and the nature of this misconduct, such as whether the experienced misconduct was done as part of a tradition, a ceremony, or joining a group.

Review of Existing Measures

Previous survey instruments can provide information regarding commonly assessed dimensions and response options provided to respondents. Therefore, when developing the instrument, the RAND team reviewed commonly used measures of hazing and bullying as a first step in the development process. To assess the fit between each measure and the military definitions of hazing and bullying, we compared existing items with the definitions contained in DoDI 1020.ef. We found that no existing measure was a precise fit to the DoD definitions, however. As such, we constructed new, military-specific measures of the percentage of service members who experience hazing and bullying each year. Although the identified measures could not be used directly, the review served as an important source of measurement strategies and lists of behaviors that may be classified as hazing and bullying. Later, after the instrument had been fielded and cognitive interviews completed, we again reviewed the literature to determine whether new measures of hazing and bullying had been developed and whether modification of the instrument might be needed.

To identify existing measures of hazing and bullying, we conducted a review of the literature. We focused on measures, written in English, of hazing and bullying among individuals aged 18 years and older. In our initial review, we limited our search to literature published between 1990 and 2017, and in our later review, we limited our search to literature published between 2017 and 2021. Although some survey measures assessed hazing and bullying perpetration, witnessing acts against others, and attitudes, we concentrated our review on measures assessing victimization experiences. For bullying measures, we focused on bullying that takes place in the workplace or on the internet (i.e., cyberbullying).

Our goal in conducting this review was to identify up to five of the most commonly used hazing measures and ten of the most commonly used bullying and cyberbullying measures. To do so, we conducted searches in Scopus, Web of Science, PsycINFO, PsycTESTS, and Google Scholar. We used several combinations of search words and phrases. For example, to identify hazing measures, we used the following: "(Hazing OR haze) AND (measur* OR questionnaire* OR survey* OR instrument* OR scale*)" with age and publication year limits. An example of a search that we conducted to identify bullying measures is "Bully* AND [restricted to title] (measur* OR questionnaire* OR survey* OR instrument* OR scale*) AND (work* OR employee* OR cyber*)" with age and publication year limits. Appendix A contains more detailed information on each of the reviewed hazing and bullying measures.

Hazing Measures

Our initial search of published survey measures identified five relevant and commonly cited instruments to assess hazing:

- the National Study of Student Hazing (Allan and Madden, 2008), which examined hazing behaviors among students in colleges and universities across the United States
- a web-based questionnaire to examine hazing among undergraduate students (Campo, Poulos, and Sipple, 2005)
- an online questionnaire to assess hazing in college marching bands (Silveira and Hudson, 2015)
- an online survey of student athletes to analyze the impact of competitive level (high school or college), gender, athletic identity, sport type, and team norms on participation in hazing and positive initiation rituals (Waldron, 2015)
- a 1990 U.S. General Accounting Office (GAO) survey of hazing among fourth-class midshipmen and cadets at the Naval Academy, the Air Force Academy, and the Military Academy (GAO, 1992).

The reasons for hazing that the measures assessed varied, with some focusing on activities conducted for initiation (Silveira and Hudson, 2015), for continuing membership (Waldron, 2015), or both (Allan and Madden, 2008; Campo, Poulos, and Sipple, 2005). The GAO, 1992, report focused on "unauthorized assumption of authority." All measures required the activities to be degrading or abusive in nature. The measures spanned in length from 9 items to more than 30 items, and psychometric properties were reported for Silveira and Hudson, 2015, and GAO, 1992, only. A summary of each instrument is included in Appendix A.

As described earlier, the five hazing instruments we reviewed were not perfectly aligned with the DoD definition of hazing. Of note, most did not differentiate hazing from behaviors that have a proper training purpose. This misalignment is not surprising in that civilian organizations do not include the types of high-stress, but mission-relevant, training experiences common in the military that could be mistaken for hazing (e.g., survival, evasion, resistance, and escape [SERE] training), and therefore, the developers did not need to untangle the two experiences. Further, no instrument captured in full the set of examples that DoD highlights in the official definition of military hazing. Therefore, we chose to create a new survey instrument of hazing that would more carefully align with a military population and the definition used by DoD. While creating a measure for DoD, we reviewed the five previous measures of hazing to inform the new measure.

New Developments in Hazing Measures

As mentioned, after the instrument had been fielded and cognitive interviews completed, we later conducted a subsequent review of the literature, using the same search terms and exclusion criteria as previously included, except for year of publication. Specifically, this new search included material published between 2017 and 2021. Our results showed that new, published research addressing hazing victimization tended to use previously developed measures already reviewed in our previous search. For example, Reid and colleagues, 2019, examined the associations between perceived consequences of hazing exposure and childhood victimization among first year college students. In doing so, they drew from the National Study of Student Hazing (Allan and Madden, 2008) to measure hazing and found that approximately 29 percent of those surveyed had experienced at least one form of hazing. In addition, Allan, Kerschner, and Payne, 2019 also drew from the same study to measure hazing experiences among college students, finding that approximately one in four survey participants who were involved in college groups (e.g., clubs, teams, and other organizations) experienced hazing.

Notably, however, Mawritz et al., 2020, published a new measure of workplace hazing, consisting of 15 items divided into five dimensions: segregation (e.g., "segregated me from our work group"), verbal abuse (e.g., "verbally embarrassed me"), task-related hazing (e.g., "gave me unimportant tasks to complete"), physical abuse (e.g., "physically harmed me"), and testing (e.g., "played pranks on me to test my gullibility"). To create the items for their measure, they drew from their own, newly developed definition of workplace hazing: "the unofficial, temporary socialization practice of initiating newcomers into workgroups by engaging in degrading behaviors toward the newcomers" (p. 5). Compared with this conceptualization, DoD's definition of hazing includes information regarding the perpetrators and the potential risks of hazing actions, and it also contains greater detail on the purpose of these acts and explicit examples of hazing acts. Thus, not surprisingly, the items that Mawritz and colleagues developed were not specific to a DoD context. For example, the items did not address whether acts were done for a work-related purpose or were performed for reasons other than official training or duties. Separately from this limited applica-bility to a DoD context, several items developed by Mawritz and colleagues also require the potential victim of hazing to make assumptions regarding the intent of the perpetrator (e.g., "told me lies to see if I am a pushover"). Based on our review of this measure, modifications to the hazing instru-ment developed for and administered by DoD were not needed.

Workplace Bullying and Cyberbullying Measures

There is an extensive literature on bullying, but the majority of this information focuses on schoolchildren. To identify measures that would be a better fit to the DoD context, we limited our review to workplace bullying among adults and cyberbullying. Our initial search identified seven relevant and commonly cited workplace bullying scales:

- the Leymann Inventory of Psychological Terrorization (LIPT; Leymann, 1990), developed to "establish the mobbing frequency in an organization"[2]
- the Work Harassment Scale (WHS; Björkqvist, Österman, and Hjelt-Bäck, 1992), developed to assess harassment between employees
- the Negative Acts Questionnaire (NAQ; Einarsen and Raknes, 1997), developed to study harassment in the workplace
- the Negative Acts Questionnaire—Revised (NAQ-R; Einarsen, Hoel, and Notelaers, 2009), developed to assess exposure to bullying in the workplace
- the Generalized Workplace Harassment Questionnaire (GWHQ; Richman et al., 1999), developed to assess experiences of harassment at work

[2] Mobbing is a type of bullying that involves the targeting of an individual by more than one person.

- the Mobbing Scale for Academic Nurses (Ozturk et al., 2008), developed by the authors to investigate experiences of mobbing among academic nurses
- the Cyberbullying Questionnaire—Victim (Gibb and Devereux, 2014), a modified version of the Cyberbullying Questionnaire by Calvete et al., 2010, focused on experiences of cyberbullying from the perspective of the victim.

We also identified two cyberbullying scales:

- the Hospital Aggressive Behaviour Scale–version Co-workers-Superiors (HABS-CS; Waschgler et al., 2013), developed to examine lateral and vertical workplace bullying behaviors among nursing staff.[3]
- the Workplace Cyberbullying Measure (WCM; Farley et al., 2016), developed to assess cyberbullying across various work settings.

Given our search criteria, all of these measures contained items that assessed behaviors in the workplace. Employee types included secondary-school teachers; university employees; nurses; athletic trainers; and Swedish, German, Japanese, French, American, Lithuanian, Finish, and Norwegian workers. The measures varied in length from 16 to 60 items, and most reported psychometric properties of the scales. A summary of each measure is included in Appendix A.

The identified measures provided useful sets of behaviorally specific items that assessed bullying and cyberbullying in the workplace. However, no single measure provided a complete set of the behaviors highlighted in the DoD definition, and some measures included items that would not be considered bullying by the military definition (e.g., "reduced opportunities to express oneself"; Björkqvist, Österman, and Hjelt-Bäck, 1994). Furthermore, published definitions and measures of bullying focus on a person experiencing a pattern, or repetition, of unpleasant action. The DoD definition of bullying does not have this requirement, making it substantially

[3] Lateral workplace bullying involves hostile behaviors by colleagues, while vertical workplace bullying involves hostile behaviors by superiors.

different from research definitions and measures of bullying found in our review. Without the requirement for a pattern or repetition of bullying behavior, individuals with a single negative experience, such as being insulted or called a hurtful name for reasons other than their official military training or duties, would be counted as having been bullied under the DoD definition. Therefore, to ensure close alignment with the DoD definition of bullying and applicability to military service members, we developed a new measure of bullying, which was informed by the work of other researchers.

New Developments in Bullying Measures

As with our subsequent search of hazing measures, we later conducted a review of the literature on bullying measures, including material published between 2017 and 2021. As with the hazing measures, our results showed that newly published research addressing bullying victimization tended to use previously developed measures already considered in our previous review. In particular, one of the most commonly cited measures continued to be the NAQ-R, and the relative frequency of this measure's use was also identified in a newly published review of measures on workplace bullying and cyberbullying (Escartin et al., 2019). For example, examining workplace bullying and work engagement, Goodboy, Martin, and Bolkan, 2020, used the NAQ-R to survey full-time employees over social media, finding that 18 percent of those sampled reporting experiencing bullying "every now and then" or more. Others translated the NAQ-R into new languages (e.g., Arabic; Makarem et al., 2018) or tested shorter versions of the measure (e.g., Anusiewicz, Li, and Patrician, 2021). We did not, however, find evidence that a new, more commonly used or highly recommended measure of workplace bullying had been developed since our previous review.

Focusing specifically on workplace cyberbullying, we found that newly published research tended to continue to use cyberbullying measures that we had previously identified and reviewed (e.g., Park and Choi, 2019). Although we found that new cyberbullying measures had been created since our previous review (e.g., Jonsson et al., 2017; Vranjes et al., 2018), researchers relatively rarely incorporated these new measures into their published research during the years of focus.

Developing Measures Tailored for the Department of Defense

Because we found that no existing measures were a precise fit to the DoD definitions, we constructed new, military-specific measures of the percentage of active-duty service members who experience hazing and bullying each year. In developing new measures, five RAND researchers with expertise in both survey development and hazing and bullying in the U.S. armed forces discussed and drafted potential items for inclusion. In drafting the survey measures, the study team had the following objectives:

- Following best practices in survey development, provide behaviorally based items.
- Align the items with the DoD definitions of hazing and bullying contained in DoDI 1020.ef.
- Limit the total number of items to roughly ten; this was at the request of the study sponsor because the measures would be included in a longer survey.

In trying to align the survey items to the DoD definitions of "hazing" and "bullying," the team drafted items that would capture the broad categories of harm described in the DoD definitions, with examples that drew from the definitions and policy to help illustrate the range of behaviors that would be included. We avoided using variants of the words "haze" and "bully" in the item wording to ensure that respondents were considering the policy definition of these behaviors rather than a preconceived or idiosyncratic definition. In addition, an important part of the DoD definition was that hazing and bullying behaviors did not have a proper training purpose because certain training experiences within the military could involve activities or behaviors that are high stress and could be mistaken for hazing-type activities (e.g., SERE training). Therefore, in the instructions and as part of certain items, we included the phrase "for reasons other than your official military training or duties."

To assess whether the behaviors would be categorized as hazing or bullying, we developed two follow-up items for respondents who had answered that they had experienced any of the behaviors identified in the initial question. To ensure that these follow-up items were behaviorally based and not reliant on respondents' idiosyncratic personal definitions of hazing and bullying, these follow-up items addressed the characteristics of hazing and bullying behaviors, rather than explicitly including the terms. To assess hazing, participants were asked for each item whether the misconduct they had indicated experiencing was "ever done as part of a tradition, ceremony, or joining a group[.] For example, it could involve a promotion ceremony, being accepted by coworkers, or starting a new job." For bullying, the DoDI definition requires only a single negative behavior for a service member to be classified as bullied. However, because the degree of repetition is critical to understanding the severity of the service members' experience, we also included an assessment of the frequency of the experience over the past 12 months in the proposed bullying measure. Though not strictly necessary, we believed that this added context would improve the interpretability of the measured prevalence of bullying. To assess the persistence of experienced behaviors and the degree of bullying, for each item a participant had indicated experiencing, they were asked, "On how many days did this happen to you?" Available response options for each survey item within this section were "1 day," "2 days," "3–9 days," "10–30 days," and "more than 30 days."

We did not include an assessment of whether the offender's bullying was done with the "intent of harming" the respondent. Given that the survey respondent would not be able to reliably ascertain the true motivation of the offender, we focused on describing the harm that occurred rather than the offender's intent.

Feedback from External Experts

Expert feedback can help to identify problems in the way survey items are worded or in the overall design of the instrument. Therefore, after developing the initial draft of our survey, we submitted the instrument to a team of academic subject-matter experts selected by RAND personnel and a group of DoD experts for review and feedback. We incorporated their recommendations to improve the survey items and design. Examples of expert-suggested changes included combining items with similar content, making revisions to reduce the required reading level, refining the instructions, and providing greater detail in programming directions. The suggested changes are also supported by research in survey design (e.g., Alwin and Beattie, 2016). Following this expert review, we submitted the instrument to OPA for inclusion in the WEO 2017 survey, at which time it was further revised by OPA.[4]

Academic Subject-Matter Expert Review

We assembled a diverse team of four experts in hazing and bullying to assist with instrument development and review. Two of our external experts, Elizabeth Allan, Ph.D., and Jennifer Waldron, Ph.D., have conducted and published multiple studies on hazing. Allan is a professor of higher education at the University of Maine College of Education and Human Development. She conducted the National Study of Student Hazing (Allan and Madden, 2008) and is the director of the National Hazing Prevention Consortium. Waldron is a professor of kinesiology at the University of Northern Iowa and has authored various articles on hazing in sports (e.g., Waldron, 2015; Waldron and Kowalski, 2009; Waldron, Lynn, and Krane, 2011).

Joel Neuman, Ph.D., and David Yamada, J.D., also served on the team as external experts in workplace bullying. Neuman is an emeritus professor of management and organizational behavior at the State University of New York at New Paltz and has published extensively on workplace aggression and violence (e.g., Neuman, 2013; Neuman and Keashly, 2013). Yamada is a professor of law and director of the New Workplace Institute at Suffolk University, Boston, and his work focuses on the legal implications of workplace bullying (e.g., Yamada, 2010).

DoD Subject-Matter Expert Review

Following instrument review and revision with the external expert team, we submitted the draft instrument for review to DoD experts. We invited representatives from DoD's ODMEO, OPA, and the Office of General Counsel to review the survey and provide their recommendations. Individuals from these offices held expertise in U.S. military equal opportunity

[4] A pretest of the survey items with a large sample of service members would allow assessment of their validity, but this fell outside the scope of this project.

policy, DoD survey administration, and legal standards of conduct involving U.S. military personnel. Expert suggestions included clarification of military policies and the referent. We responded to each of their comments and incorporated their suggestions as appropriate.

Submission of Initial Draft

In May 2017, the RAND team submitted the recommended survey instrument to OPA for inclusion in the 2017 WEO survey (see Appendix B for a revised version of this instrument). Before fielding the survey, the OPA team modified the instrument design (contained in Appendix C). As shown in Appendix B, the authors recommended that each bullying or hazing behavior the respondent said that he or she experienced be followed immediately by questions to assess whether the experience could be classified as hazing and the frequency with which it occurred. We expected that this would reduce the cognitive burden placed on respondents (i.e., working memory load) by allowing them to focus on one behavior at a time, rather than potentially repeatedly addressing a diverse set of behaviors (Lenzer, Kaczmirek, and Lenzner, 2010).

Office of People Analytics Modification and Implementation of Survey Module

The OPA-revised version (Appendix C) restructures the survey to first present items addressing the full series of hazing and bullying behaviors. Then, for all endorsed items, the instrument presents a table to assess whether each was hazing and a subsequent table to assess the frequency with which it occurred. This structure was revised with the goal of facilitating ease of programming. However, the redesign might increase the cognitive demands on participants and increase the risk of biased prevalence estimates caused by reading and comprehension errors. OPA also added two items to the instrument, which were intended to remain in the instrument beyond initial implementation: an open-ended item requesting information about the characteristics of the experience and a yes/no item addressing online behaviors. The OPA-revised version of the survey instrument was fielded as part of the 2017 WEO survey.

Summary

Upon a review of the hazing and bullying literature, we found no existing measures that were a precise fit to the DoD definitions. Therefore, we constructed new, military-specific measures of the percentage of active-duty service members who experience hazing and bullying each year. In developing the new measures, the research team drew on the previous measures we had reviewed, as well as expert feedback obtained, to help refine the final draft measure used in cognitive interviews.

CHAPTER THREE

Cognitive Interviews with Service Members

Cognitive interviewing is a widely used method in survey development that allows researchers to examine how participants interpret survey instructions, items, and response options (Willis, 2005). Cognitive interviews are used to explore how participants understand survey items, what information they recall or consider when answering an item, and how they decide to respond to a survey item. The information obtained from these interviews can be used to correct unclear item wording and structural limitations within a survey that could have produced response errors (Willis, 2005). To ensure greater clarity of the instrument instructions and items, the RAND team conducted cognitive interviews with 27 active-duty service members using the DoD-revised instrument that OPA fielded as part of the 2017 Workplace and Equal Opportunity Survey of Active Duty (WEOA) (see Appendix C). This chapter summarizes the feedback that we received during these interviews and, where applicable, subsequent changes made to the instrument following review of this feedback by a team of five RAND researchers.

Participants

From June 2018 through October 2018, we conducted cognitive interviews with a total of 27 participants. To obtain diverse perspectives, we sought to interview people within each cell of a 4 (military service) × 2 (gender) × 2 (personnel category) design matrix. Specifically, we sought to interview male and female active-duty officers and enlisted personnel in each U.S. military service—Army, Navy, Air Force, and Marine Corps. To identify participants, an ODMEO staff member requested assistance from a number of service-specific Military Equal Opportunity representatives. Those individuals then requested volunteers for the cognitive interviews and provided the contact information of volunteers to ODMEO and then to RAND. As such, the RAND team was limited to recruiting only those who had informed their service representatives that they would be willing to participate.

To recruit participants from the list of volunteers, one of two possible RAND researchers sent an initial email to a potential participant. This email contained information regarding the study, purpose of the interviews, voluntary nature of the task, and approximate time required to complete each interview. In the email, each researcher asked whether the individual would be interested and available to participate in an interview and attached a copy of the informed consent. If an individual did not respond to this initial email within approximately one week, the researcher sent a reminder email regarding the request, and if the individual did not respond within approximately one week after this reminder, the researcher sent a final reminder email. If an individual did not respond approximately one week after this final request, the researcher then moved to contacting another individual who had volunteered to participate. Forty-two percent of the invited service members scheduled and completed an interview. Table 3.1 provides a summary of participant characteristics.

After an individual informed the researcher that he or she was interested and available to participate in an interview, the researcher worked with the participant to establish a mutually agreed-on date and time for a telephone interview. In addition, each researcher provided the individual with another copy of the informed consent and a PDF of the draft hazing and bullying

TABLE 3.1
Cognitive Interview Sample Characteristics

	Army		Navy		Air Force		Marine Corps	
Category	Male	Female	Male	Female	Male	Female	Male	Female
Enlisted	1	3	2	2	2	2	2	1
Officer	1	0	2	2	2	2	2	1

NOTES: Enlisted personnel were approximately evenly divided between those in ranks E4 and lower and those in ranks E5 and higher. Officers were approximately evenly divided between those in ranks O3 and lower and those in ranks O4 and higher.

survey items for review. The researcher asked the individual to assess each survey item as if he or she were another active-duty military member (i.e., imagine how someone else would respond). Participants were asked not to send their survey responses to the researcher or anyone else.

Cognitive Interview Methods

The same researcher who had contacted the participant via email conducted the interview with the participant using retrospective verbal probing (Willis, 2005). Probes included open-ended questions such as the following:

- Were there any words or phrases that were unclear?
- How did you interpret the phrase "[target phrase]"?
- Can you give examples of the types of experiences that might cause people to say "yes"?
- Can you give examples of things that people might have experienced but would not "count" to answer a "yes"?
- How did you decide on a response option to this question?

The researcher conducting each interview recorded the participant's response to each question. The time to complete each interview ranged from 30 to 60 minutes, depending on the amount of feedback provided by a participant.

After completion of the cognitive interviews, a team of five RAND researchers then reviewed participants' feedback by section and item, discussing participants' comments and options for revision. A consensus among the team of researchers established whether to incorporate instruction and item changes and how best to do so.

Findings

Section-by-Section Instructions

Cognitive interviewees described their interpretation of the instructions provided before each instrument section—namely, the instructions before Question 22, Question 24, and Question 25 (see Table 3.2 and Appendix C).

TABLE 3.2

Changes to Instrument, Section, and Question Instructions

Location in Survey	Original Instruction	Revised Instruction	Summary of Changes
Instrument instructions	The following questions ask about things that happened within the past 12 months. For these items, "military member" may refer to anyone in your chain of command, including DoD civilians.	The following questions ask about things that happened within the past 12 months. For these items, "service member" refers to members of the Active and Reserve Components.	Changed "military member" to "service member" and defined "service member"
Question 22 instructions	Since [X date], did a military member . . .	Since [X date], did a service member or civilian working for the military . . .	Changed "military member" to "service member or civilian working for the military"
Question 24 section instructions (revised Question 23)	You indicated in the previous questions that within the past 12 months you experienced behaviors from a military member. The following questions ask about the purpose of the misconduct.	In the previous questions, you described experiences that happened within the past 12 months. The following questions ask about the purpose.	Revised structure to avoid use of "military member" and "misconduct"
Question 24 instructions (revised Question 23)	Since [X date], was this misconduct ever done as part of a tradition, ceremony, or joining a group? For example, it could involve a promotion ceremony, being accepted by coworkers, or starting a new job.	Since [X date], was this ever done as part of a tradition, ceremony, or joining a group? For example, it could involve a promotion ceremony, being accepted by coworkers, or starting a new job.	Removed the word "misconduct"
Question 25 section instructions (revised Question 24)	You indicated in the previous questions that within the past 12 months you experienced behaviors from a military member. The following questions ask about the frequency that these behaviors occurred.	In the previous questions, you described experiences that happened within the past 12 months. The following questions ask about how often they happened.	Revised structure to avoid use of "military member"
Question 25 instructions (revised Question 24)	Since [X date], on how many days did this happen to you? A military member . . .	Since [X date], on how many days did this happen to you? A service member or civilian working for the military . . .	Changed "military member" to "service member or civilian working for the military"

Military Member

The instrument instructions described a military member as "anyone in your chain of command, including DoD civilians" (see Table 3.2). Participants were asked to describe their interpretation of a military member based on these instructions. Although the description of the term included "DoD civilians," many participants did not consider DoD civilians to be military members. For example, one participant noted, "When I see 'military member,' I think of someone who is in uniform, even though you indicate DoD civilians too. I only think of those who wear the uniform. When I look at it, whenever we say 'military member,' I think [of] anyone in uniform, not civilians" (Air Force, enlisted).

DoD civilians could perpetrate bullying or hazing against service members, so their actions should also be considered by those who complete the survey. To improve clarity, we changed all references to "a military member" to read instead "a service member or civilian working for the military." We also modified the instrument instructions to clarify that "service member" refers to members of the Active and Reserve Components.

Misconduct as Part of a Tradition, Ceremony, or Joining a Group

The instructions for Question 24 asked participants whether "misconduct" they had indicated experiencing within Question 22 was "ever done as part of a tradition, ceremony, or joining a group[.] For example, it could involve a promotion ceremony, being accepted by coworkers, or starting a new job." Cognitive interview participants were asked to describe categories of events they believed that these instructions captured.

Participants commented that the instructions were clear, and often described events that were intended to be captured by these instructions. One individual commented, "So with this one, it's 'did all this happen as sort of a rite of passage?' We talked about the pinning and blood striping for promotion ceremonies" (Marine Corps, officer). Another person stated, "When you say being accepted, there are certain things you have to [do] to become a chief. If you don't go through the initiation for being a chief, then you are blacklisted in the community. . . . Some things are official, some things aren't" (Navy, enlisted).

Based on their responses, participants appeared to interpret the instruction as intended. Therefore, we largely maintained the question instructions. However, we removed the word "misconduct" from the instructions for Question 24 and throughout the survey. This word placed a negative evaluation on the behaviors, reducing survey neutrality; was grammatically unnecessary; and may have reduced respondents' willingness to disclose hazing rituals in which they voluntarily participated.

Number of Days Experienced

To assess the persistence of experienced behaviors, Question 25 asked participants, "On how many days did this happen to you?" Available response options for each survey item within this section were "1 day," "2 days," "3–9 days," "10–30 days," and "more than 30 days." Participants were asked to describe their interpretation of the available response options.

Participants provided similar interpretations regarding how they would respond using the response options. One person stated, "The survey says on how many days did this happen to you. If it happened on one day, I will say one day, even if it was a lot of things on that one day" (Air Force, enlisted). Another commented, "The way I interpreted this is, basically, how many days. If there was one instance on one day, that would be one day. If it was multiple instances on one day, that's one day. If it was two instances over two weeks, I would interpret that as two days" (Marine Corps, officer). Drawing from participants' responses, the instructions and response options appeared to be interpreted as we had intended. As such, we did not make modifications to the question instructions.

Item Review

Question 22, Question 24, and Question 25 contained the same survey subitems, such that the item wording for each question was the same, but the instructions listed before each question's section varied (see earlier discussion and Appendix C). To reduce participant fatigue, cognitive interviewees were not asked to discuss the same items three times, once for each section. Rather, participants were asked to discuss each item in Question 22 (Table 3.3). After that, they were asked to skim the items in Question 24 and

TABLE 3.3

Item Wording for First Question Set Presented to Participants

Location in Survey	Original Item Example	Revised Item Example	Summary of Changes
Questions 22d, 23d, 24d	**Harmfully trick or abuse you** for reasons other than your official military training or duties? For example, they intentionally left you stranded, or bound, taped, shaved, or painted your body.	**Subject you to a cruel prank or abuse you** for reasons other than your official military training or duties? For example, they intentionally left you stranded, or bound, taped, shaved, or painted your body.	Changed "harmfully trick" to "subject you to a cruel prank"
Questions 22g, 23g, 24g	**Try to humiliate you** for reasons other than your official military training or duties? For example, they shared nude pictures without your permission, spread hurtful gossip about you online, or made you pretend to have sex.	**Try to humiliate you** for reasons other than your official military training or duties? For example, they shared nude pictures without your permission, spread hurtful gossip about you, or made you do something embarrassing.	Removed "online" to include all hurtful gossip and changed last example to nonsexual example
Questions 22h, 23h, 24h	**Hurtfully insult you** for reasons other than your official military training or duties? For example, they made fun of your appearance or tried to upset you by calling you a fag or dyke.	**Hurtfully insult you** for reasons other than your official military training or duties? For example, they made fun of your appearance or tried to upset you by calling you a fag or retard.	Changed example from "dyke" to "retard" to prompt recall of a broader range of insults
Questions 22j, 23j, 24j	**Touch your private body parts, or make you touch theirs, when they knew this contact was unwanted?** For example, they pressed their crotch on you, put something in your rectum, or groped you.	**Touch your private body parts, or make you touch theirs, when they knew this contact was unwanted** for reasons other than your official military training or duties? For example, they pressed their crotch on you, put something in your rectum, or groped you.	Included reference to reasons other than official military duties; removed Question 23

provide any additional comments or changes, based on the new instructions for the question. They were again asked to do this for items in Question 25. Next, we describe comments made in response to instrument items. Generally, we focus on items that required wording changes.

Reasons Other Than Official Military Training or Duties

Many items within the instrument addressed whether individuals experienced negative behaviors "for reasons other than your official military training or duties." This phrase was designed to ensure that unpleasant but sanctioned training experiences (e.g., SERE training) were not incorrectly counted as bullying or hazing incidents against service members. Given the role of this phrase in excluding unpleasant sanctioned experiences, it was important to verify that participants interpreted the phrase as we had intended. Participants provided a variety of responses, and, overall, these comments suggested a common interpretation of the phrase. For example, one person stated, "Um, [it's] like anything that's unnecessary. Things that don't have to deal with performing your job or getting your mission done" (Army, enlisted). Another commented, "That would mean, um, if I wasn't in any training or on duty or working. They shouldn't be doing it for the fun of it. It should have a defendable reason—as part of training or duties—it should have a defendable reason" (Air Force, officer). These and similar comments suggested that individuals interpreted this phrase as intended. Therefore, no changes were made to the phrase. In addition, to ensure clarity and a common understanding across items, the phrase was maintained in most survey items.

Harmfully Trick or Abuse You

Item D within Questions 22, 24, and 25 described the following behavior: "Harmfully trick[ed] or abuse[d] you for reasons other than your official military training or duties? For example, they intentionally left you stranded, or bound, taped, shaved, or painted your body." When discussing the wording of this item, several participants noted that they were confused by the use of the word "trick." One individual commented, "It's the 'harmfully trick,' the word 'trick.' I don't know what I would change it to. I do understand the intent of the question . . . but I don't really know what 'trick' means. Maybe a different way of describing that" (Marine Corps, officer). An additional person noted, "From my experience in the Marine Corps, I know these things . . . have occurred for both reasons of hazing and simple pranks. Someone could be pranked or abused. I think pranked is maybe a better word. Trick seems like something you would do with cards" (Marine Corps, enlisted). Drawing from the feedback we received, we replaced the phrase "Harmfully trick[ed]" with "Subject[ed] you to a cruel prank."

Try to Humiliate You

Item G within Questions 22, 24, and 25 contained the following wording: "[Try/Tried] to humiliate you for reasons other than your official military training or duties? For example, they shared nude pictures without your permission, spread hurtful gossip about you online, or made you pretend to have sex." Several participants questioned the provided examples. One person stated, "I'm not sure how the examples tie into the original question. The examples are all sexual in nature or could be perceived as that, but the question isn't. Either the question doesn't fit the examples, or the examples don't fit the question" (Marine Corps, officer). Another individual commented, "Made you pretend to have sex—I don't know anything about that" (Navy, enlisted).

To improve item clarity, we modified the examples provided with Item G. We removed the example "made you pretend to have sex" and replaced it with "made you do something embarrassing." This new phrase addresses a broader range of possible behaviors. In addition, we removed "online" from the example "spread hurtful gossip about you online" to encourage participants to consider both online and offline behaviors.

Hurtfully Insult You

Item H within Questions 22, 24, and 25 used the following wording: "Hurtfully insult[ed] you for reasons other than your official military training or duties? For example, they made fun of your appearance or tried to upset you by calling you a fag or dyke." In discussing this item, participants tended to focus on the provided examples, often suggesting maintaining the example slurs and also including additional slurs. One individual commented, "I think that happens, but there's a lot of other names. To only have the homosexual pejoratives, you might only get those things" (Air Force, officer). An additional person noted, "It's accurate. . . . Don't take 'fag or dyke' out of it, but possibly add race, religion or ethnicity, or something like that" (Navy, officer).

To address participant comments, we removed the term "dyke." This was done to reduce emphasis on sexual orientation, as suggested by participants. We replaced it with the slur "retard" to maintain the severity of the insult while also broadening the examples to include other types of slurs.

Touch Your Private Body Parts and Follow Up

Item J contained the following wording: "Touch your private body parts, or make you touch theirs, when they knew this contact was unwanted? For example, they pressed their crotch on you, put something in your rectum, or groped you." Those who responded "yes" to Item J in Question 22 would then receive Question 23. Question 23 read, "You indicated a military member touched your private body parts, or made you touch his/hers, when he/she knew this contact was unwanted. Was this part of an official medical exam or for [an]other official military purpose?" This follow-up question was intended to rule out permissible touching during medical procedures that turn out to be unwanted by the respondent (e.g., a rectal thermometer used to monitor body temperature of an unconscious heat-stroke victim). During the cognitive interviews, participants indicated confusion regarding the purpose of Question 23. The following comment is representative of the types of confusion we heard:

> That's not flowing well to me. They already indicated that it was unwanted. . . . When you use examples of "press their crotch on you" or "groped you," I can't see that as part of an official medical exam. I don't know a better way to word this. I could see touching private body parts as part of a medical exam or putting something in your rectum. But someone pressing their crotch on you [or] groping you, that's never a medical necessity. (Air Force, enlisted)

Another respondent expressed concern that misinterpretation of Question 23 could lead to mistakenly ruling out sexual assaults by medical professionals: "There have been claims of people being sexually assaulted by medical professionals. [It] can't just be 'part of an official medical exam,' should be 'part of an appropriate official medical exam'" (Air Force, officer). To reduce confusion, we removed Question 23 and instead added the exclusion phrase "for reasons other than your official military duties" to Item J.

Concluding Survey Questions

As explained previously, DoD included two additional questions within the survey instrument after those that had been developed by RAND researchers and reviewed by survey experts. Cognitive interviewees reviewed and provided comments on these two additional DoD-developed questions.

Specify Context

The penultimate survey question was worded as follows:

> In the previous question you indicated experiencing a behavior from a military member. Please specify in what context this behavior occurred (e.g., during training, with a supervisor present). Please do not include any Personally Identifiable Information (PII) that could identify yourself or others.

The item prompt was followed by a free-text response box to allow survey respondents to write in their answer. Several cognitive interviewees expressed concerns regarding this survey question, with many specifically questioning how the data would be used. For example, some were unsure how this question would be used for research purposes. One person stated, "How will you analyze this? Do you have text searching capabilities? When we do surveys, the question is how will you use the data once collected? If the answer is 'we don't really know how,' then maybe remove it. Don't make someone answer it if you can't analyze it" (Marine Corps, officer).

Other concerns focused on how confidentiality would be maintained. One individual commented, "Just describing the situation would tip my hand to someone in my organization who is going to see it" (Army, officer). Another commented, "I don't think they could say much, because it will affect the person. If you put anything—even gender—for people who are going to read the comments, the person will think of who did this. Maybe it will lead someone to get in trouble, and they'll wonder who said something bad. And they'll know who wrote on the survey" (Army, enlisted).

Finally, several cognitive interviewees questioned whether participants would have the time or inclination to provide detailed comments, and they suggested instead including a series of multiple-choice questions to address context. One individual stated,

> [No PII] means no names, no rank. That kind of takes away from the entire question. If you want people to put what happened to them, it would be hard for them to leave out those details. It should be a multiple choice—like supervisor present, supervisor not present; during training, outside of training—things like that. If I felt like I was being hazed and couldn't put PII, I'd just put "at work" and move on. (Navy, enlisted)

Comments from cognitive interviewees suggest that, rather than a text box, which introduces confidentiality and data analysis challenges, DoD should consider using a series of multiple-choice questions to capture the contextual elements of interest. These questions might draw from, for example, those used in the RAND Military Workplace Survey (National Defense Research Institute, 2014).

Online Misconduct

The final survey question contained the following wording:

> Did any of the behaviors you indicated experiencing from a military member include online misconduct (e.g., social media posts, unsolicited contact through the internet)?

DoD's proposed programming instructions indicated that, for the final online survey version, this question was to be presented to those who responded "yes" to any item in Question 22 and, for those who responded "yes" to Item J, those who also responded "no" to Question 23.

Three of the behaviors described in Question 22 are specific to an in-person context, rather than online context. Specifically, deprivation of food, water, or sleep (Item B); damaging property (Item E); and touching private parts (Item J) cannot occur online. Several participants noted this disconnect between the previous survey items and question assessing whether the behavior occurred online. For example, one individual commented, "What about [the] sexual contact item? It can't happen online. Seems like a weird thing. You're going along, answering the questions, and then you get this really strange question. Seems like it would throw you off and make you think you weren't being listened to" (Air Force, officer). Another stated, "The last question seems out of place. Causing you pain, depriving you of food, pressuring you to drink, that happens in person. If you're trying to get into cyber bullying, have more follow-on questions. It seems out of place" (Army, enlisted).

Drawing from participant comments, we recommend that individuals who only responded "yes" to Item B, Item E, or Item J not be asked to complete this follow-up question. We have included this proposed programming in the final survey instrument in Chapter Four.

Additional Comments

In addition to comments on item and instruction wording, participants also provided comments regarding the survey overall.

Survey Structure

Some of these comments addressed survey structure. For example, when reviewing the table of items (Question 24) that determine whether the original behaviors (Question 22) were part of a hazing ritual, an individual noted,

> It looks like the same question that you just answered. What if someone doesn't read the instructions? Could there be an immediate pop-up that asks about whether it was a tradition [or] ceremony, so that you're still on the same topic? The way it is now, you'll be toggling back and forth from topic to topic and having to remember/revisit what you said before. Why not just ask them about the tradition or ceremony while they're already thinking about it? (Navy, officer)

Before the DoD restructure of the instrument, the survey was designed in the same way this respondent suggests (see Appendix B). That is, respondents who indicate that they experienced a particular negative behavior are then immediately prompted with follow-up items about whether the behavior occurred as part of a hazing ritual and the frequency with which it occurred. This strategy was approved by survey development experts internal and external to RAND as a survey design strategy that reduces the cognitive load of respondents and increases the ease with which they can respond to items.

The DoD-restructured format that cognitive interviewees reviewed might increase cognitive load for the follow-up questions by requiring participants to reorient to the specified behavior twice in subsequent question tables (Goldstein, 2014). In addition, if participants skip or forget the item stem, it looks like the original screening items (Question 22) are simply being repeated. Therefore, some participants might interpret the hazing follow-up table (Question 24) as the same items again, leading either to incorrect responses or to ending the survey early because of frustration or anger.

If participants incorrectly respond to Question 24, assuming that it is a repeat of Question 22, a large portion of respondents will be categorized as experiencing hazing, which will inflate the hazing prevalence estimate in error. Because cognitive interviewing requires close review and detailed responses to survey questions by participants, responses from cognitive interviewees do not permit us to comment on whether survey respondents would misinterpret the table this way in real-world conditions. To assess this possibility, the OPA team should review the observed hazing rate, considering whether inflation in the observed rate could be due to item misinterpretation. For example, if nearly all respondents indicate that the negative experience was part of an initiation, it is possible that they were agreeing that the event happened rather than noting that it was hazing. Absent this additional information, the authors suggest use of the instrument format originally provided to OPA following expert review (see Appendix B).

Overall Impressions

Some survey items include concrete descriptions of sexual assault and example slurs that could upset some participants when they read the item. To assess whether this occurred, at the conclusion of each cognitive interview, participants were asked whether they found the survey or any particular questions upsetting and whether there were any words or questions that embarrassed or offended them. Cognitive interviewees did not indicate that they felt personally upset by the survey or particular questions in the survey. In addition, none of the interviewees indicated that they were embarrassed or offended by words or questions in the survey. However, participants did note that certain terms were unexpected or surprising. For example, one individual commented, "No. It was surprising to see that you referenced the two names—I'll just say them, 'fag' and 'dyke.' Like I said, those words are not acceptable in the Marine Corps. To see them on the paper, it was surprising, but I wouldn't say it was upsetting" (Marine Corps, officer). As noted previously, we modified the example slurs in Item H to reduce the emphasis on sexual orientation, while also maintaining behaviorally specific examples.

Summary

Cognitive interviews are one avenue that survey designers use to identify possible interpretation errors in self-report surveys and improve survey instruments. Therefore, RAND researchers conducted cognitive interviews with service members to gain initial insights into how a respondent might interpret various words and phrases and respond to items. This information facilitated modifications to improve the clarity and comprehension of instrument instructions and items.

Following incorporation of these modifications, time and resource constraints did not allow us to conduct additional cognitive testing on the revised survey, however. This additional testing would have allowed us to explore whether the incorporated modifications adequately addressed issues raised by the first set of cognitive interviewees.

CHAPTER FOUR

Department of Defense–Revised Bullying and Hazing Instrument Following Incorporation of Cognitive Interview Recommendations

The instrument design with all recommended edits from the cognitive interviews, including coding instructions and programming notes, is provided in this chapter. The instrument follows the version of the instrument that DoD restructured (see Appendix C for more information). It has been designed so that participants first address whether they experienced broad classes of harm or risks of harm. Then, they address characteristics of these experiences. Specifically, the first survey items, contained in the table for Question 22, can be considered screener items that capture whether a class of harm or risk of harm was experienced but not whether this occurred during an incident of hazing or bullying. Many survey participants will only complete the items contained in Question 22. If an individual responds "yes" to an item in Question 22, he or she will receive follow-up questions. These follow-up questions establish whether the harms constitute hazing (Questions 23) and the frequency of the harm (Question 24). DoD developed and added Questions 25 and 26. Based on comments received during cognitive interviews, the RAND team has modified the programming structure for these items. Throughout, all questions have been numbered based on their expected location within DoD's next administration of the WEOA survey instrument.

As noted in Chapter Three, the following survey structure might be cognitively burdensome for participants. Placement of follow-up items regarding each category of behavior immediately following that category of behavior would reduce the cognitive burden. For example, immediately after a participant responds "yes" to one item in Question 22, he or she would then receive a follow-up question regarding behavioral intent to bring the individual into or include him or her in a group and a second follow-up question regarding persistence. For an example of this structure, see Appendix B.

Instrument Structure Following Incorporation of Comments from Cognitive Interviews

Coding Instructions

Bullying

In concordance with draft DoDI 1020.ef, a service member who responds "yes" to any of the screening items Q22a through Q22j should be classified as possibly experiencing bullying in the past year. That is,

Bullying = TRUE if
- Q22a = 1 (yes) OR
- Q22b = 1 (yes) OR
- Q22c = 1 (yes) OR
- Q22d = 1 (yes) OR
- Q22e = 1 (yes) OR
- Q22f = 1 (yes) OR
- Q22g = 1 (yes) OR
- Q22h = 1 (yes) OR
- Q22i = 1 (yes) OR
- Q22j = 1 (yes)

Persistent Bullying

Being classified as "bullied" does not require any specific response on follow-up items in Question 24. The frequency follow-up items (all items in

Question 24) are included to provide important contextual information. Because DoDI 1020.ef does not require events to occur more than a single time to be classified as bullying, we expect that the prevalence of bullying in the armed forces will be high. In response to the expected high-prevalence estimates, we believe that leaders and decisionmakers will want clarification regarding the meaning of the estimate. Example questions include "Is there an epidemic of bullying in the military? Or do these data describe concerning but one-time events?" Although not strictly necessary to measure DoD-defined bullying, DoD may wish to have frequency data available to support an empirical response to the expected questions. Alternatively, it may choose to select a criterion for classification of "persistent bullying" and present that estimate alongside a bullying estimate. As an example, the following quasi-programming code sets specifications for persistent bullying using events that occurred on three or more days as the criterion.

```
PersistentBullying = TRUE if
    (Q22a = 1 (yes) AND Q24a = (3 OR 4 OR 5)) OR
    (Q22b = 1 (yes) AND Q24b = (3 OR 4 OR 5)) OR
    (Q22c = 1 (yes) AND Q24c = (3 OR 4 OR 5)) OR
    (Q22d = 1 (yes) AND Q24d = (3 OR 4 OR 5)) OR
    (Q22e = 1 (yes) AND Q24e = (3 OR 4 OR 5)) OR
    (Q22f = 1 (yes) AND Q24f = (3 OR 4 OR 5)) OR
    (Q22g = 1 (yes) AND Q24g = (3 OR 4 OR 5)) OR
    (Q22h = 1 (yes) AND Q24h = (3 OR 4 OR 5)) OR
    (Q22i = 1 (yes) AND Q24i = (3 OR 4 OR 5)) OR
    (Q22j = 1 (yes) AND Q24j = (3 OR 4 OR 5))
```

Hazing

As defined in draft DoDI 1020.ef, some bullying may also be hazing. That is, if a bullying incident occurs, it may *also* be hazing if the purpose of the misconduct was for "initiation into, admission into, affiliation with, change in status or position within, or as a condition for continued membership in any military or Department of Defense civilian organization." Therefore, service members should be classified as having experienced hazing in the past year if they respond "yes" to any screening item and *also* respond "yes" to the follow-up item assessing the intent to bring into or include them in a group. That is,

Hazing = TRUE if
(Q22a = 1 (yes) AND Q23a = 1 (yes)) OR
(Q22b = 1 (yes) AND Q23b = 1 (yes)) OR
(Q22c = 1 (yes) AND Q23c = 1 (yes)) OR
(Q22d = 1 (yes) AND Q23d = 1 (yes)) OR
(Q22e = 1 (yes) AND Q23e = 1 (yes)) OR
(Q22f = 1 (yes) AND Q23f = 1 (yes)) OR
(Q22g = 1 (yes) AND Q23g = 1 (yes)) OR
(Q22h = 1 (yes) AND Q23h = 1 (yes)) OR
(Q22i = 1 (yes) AND Q23i = 1 (yes)) OR
(Q22j = 1 (yes) AND Q23j = 1 (yes))

All service members who are classified as "hazed" should *also* be classified as "bullied."

Programming Notes

Programming notes are in blue.
Variable labels and coding values are in red.

- Optimize the questionnaire for smartphone use.
- Limit the screen width of question text for readability.
- Unless specified otherwise, all participants get each question.
- Questions and response options should be in regular type.
- Present follow-up instructions for each screener in the top center of the screen and on the same page as all follow-up questions for that screener.

"X date" is the month, day, and year that is one year prior to the date on which the participant began the survey. Set "X date" when the participant answers the consent question and keep that date no matter when they return during fielding.

Instrument

The following questions ask about things that happened within the past 12 months. For these items, "service member" refers to military members of the Active and Reserve Components.

Q22. **Since [X date], did a service member or civilian working for the military . . .** ***Mark "Yes" or "No" for each item.***

	Yes	No
Q22a. **Threaten or deliberately cause you physical pain** for reasons other than your official military training or duties? For example, they pinned insignia into your skin, or hit, kicked, pushed, or slapped you.	1 ☐	2 ☐
Q22b. **Deprive you of food, water, or sleep** for reasons other than your official military training or duties?	1 ☐	2 ☐
Q22c. **Pressure you to consume harmful amounts of alcohol, water, or other substances** for reasons other than your official military training or duties?	1 ☐	2 ☐
Q22d. **Subject you to a cruel prank or abuse you** for reasons other than your official military training or duties? For example, they intentionally left you stranded, or bound, taped, shaved, or painted your body.	1 ☐	2 ☐
Q22e. **Take or damage your property** for reasons other than your official military training or duties?	1 ☐	2 ☐
Q22f. **Pressure you to do something illegal or dangerous** for reasons other than your official military training or duties? For example, they pressured you to take risks to prove your bravery, steal something, or harm another person.	1 ☐	2 ☐
Q22g. **Try to humiliate you** for reasons other than your official military training or duties? For example, they shared nude pictures without your permission, spread hurtful gossip about you, or made you do something embarrassing.	1 ☐	2 ☐
Q22h. **Hurtfully insult you** for reasons other than your official military training or duties? For example, they made fun of your appearance or tried to upset you by calling you a fag or retard.	1 ☐	2 ☐
Q22i. **Pressure you to engage in disgusting activities** for reasons other than your official military training or duties? For example, put something gross in your mouth, threw you in unsanitary water, or encouraged you to urinate on someone.	1 ☐	2 ☐
Q22j. **Touch your private body parts, or make you touch theirs, when they knew this contact was unwanted** for reasons other than your official military training or duties? For example, they pressed their crotch on you, put something in your rectum, or groped you.	1 ☐	2 ☐

[Participants who responded "No" to all items in Q22 will skip all remaining items. After completing items Q22a through Q22j, participants who responded "Yes" to any one of the items in Q22a through Q22j will receive the corresponding items in Q23 and Q24. If they responded "No" to an item in Q22a through Q22j, they will not receive the corresponding item in Q23 and Q24. For example, if a participant responds "Yes" to Q22a, they will receive Q23a and Q24a. If they respond "No" to Q22a, they will not receive Q23a or Q24a.]

In the previous questions, you described experiences that happened within the past 12 months. The following questions ask about the purpose.

Q23. **Since [X date], was this ever done as part of a tradition, ceremony, or joining a group? For example, it could involve a promotion ceremony, being accepted by coworkers, or starting a new job.**

A service member or civilian working for the military . . . ***Mark "Yes" or "No" for each item.***

	Yes	No
Q23a. **Threatened or deliberately caused you physical pain** for reasons other than your official military training or duties? For example, they pinned insignia into your skin, or hit, kicked, pushed, or slapped you.	1 ☐	2 ☐
Q23b. **Deprived you of food, water, or sleep** for reasons other than your official military training or duties?	1 ☐	2 ☐
Q23c. **Pressured you to consume harmful amounts of alcohol, water, or other substances** for reasons other than your official military training or duties?	1 ☐	2 ☐
Q23d. **Subjected you to a cruel prank or abused you** for reasons other than your official military training or duties? For example, he/she intentionally left you stranded, or bound, taped, shaved, or painted your body.	1 ☐	2 ☐
Q23e. **Took or damaged your property** for reasons other than your official military training or duties?	1 ☐	2 ☐
Q23f. **Pressured you to do something illegal or dangerous** for reasons other than your official military training or duties? For example, he/she pressured you to take risks to prove your bravery, steal something, or harm another person.	1 ☐	2 ☐
Q23g. **Tried to humiliate you** for reasons other than your official military training or duties? For example, he/she shared nude pictures without your permission, spread hurtful gossip about you, or made you do something embarrassing.	1 ☐	2 ☐
Q23h. **Hurtfully insulted you** for reasons other than your official military training or duties? For example, he/she made fun of your appearance or tried to upset you by calling you a fag or retard.	1 ☐	2 ☐
Q23i. **Pressured you to engage in disgusting activities** for reasons other than your official military training or duties? For example, put something gross in your mouth, threw you in unsanitary water, or encouraged you to urinate on someone.	1 ☐	2 ☐
Q23j. **Touched your private body parts, or made you touch theirs, when they knew this contact was unwanted** for reasons other than your official military training or duties.	1 ☐	2 ☐

In the previous questions, you described experiences that happened within the past 12 months. The following questions ask about how often they happened.

Q24. **Since [X date], on how many days did this happen to you?**

A service member or civilian working for the military . . . ***Mark one answer for each item.***

	More than 30 days	10–30 days	3–9 days	2 days	1 day
Q24a. **Threatened or deliberately caused you physical pain** for reasons other than your official military training or duties? For example, they pinned insignia into your skin, or hit, kicked, pushed, or slapped you.	5 ☐	4 ☐	3 ☐	2 ☐	1 ☐
Q24b. **Deprived you of food, water, or sleep** for reasons other than your official military training or duties?	5 ☐	4 ☐	3 ☐	2 ☐	1 ☐
Q24c. **Pressured you to consume harmful amounts of alcohol, water, or other substances** for reasons other than your official military training or duties?	5 ☐	4 ☐	3 ☐	2 ☐	1 ☐
Q24d. **Subjected you to a cruel prank or abused you** for reasons other than your official military training or duties? For example, he/she intentionally left you stranded, or bound, taped, shaved, or painted your body.	5 ☐	4 ☐	3 ☐	2 ☐	1 ☐
Q24e. **Took or damaged your property** for reasons other than your official military training or duties?	5 ☐	4 ☐	3 ☐	2 ☐	1 ☐
Q24f. **Pressured you to do something illegal or dangerous** for reasons other than your official military training or duties? For example, he/she pressured you to take risks to prove your bravery, steal something, or harm another person.	5 ☐	4 ☐	3 ☐	2 ☐	1 ☐
Q24g. **Tried to humiliate you** for reasons other than your official military training or duties? For example, he/she shared nude pictures without your permission, spread hurtful gossip about you, or made you do something embarrassing.	5 ☐	4 ☐	3 ☐	2 ☐	1 ☐
Q24h. **Hurtfully insulted you** for reasons other than your official military training or duties? For example, he/she made fun of your appearance or tried to upset you by calling you a fag or retard.	5 ☐	4 ☐	3 ☐	2 ☐	1 ☐
Q24i. **Pressured you to engage in disgusting activities** for reasons other than your official military training or duties? For example, put something gross in your mouth, threw you in unsanitary water, or encouraged you to urinate on someone.	5 ☐	4 ☐	3 ☐	2 ☐	1 ☐
Q24j. **Touched your private body parts, or made you touch theirs, when they knew this contact was unwanted** for reasons other than your official military training or duties.	5 ☐	4 ☐	3 ☐	2 ☐	1 ☐

[After completing Q23 and Q24, participants who responded "Yes" to any one of the items in Q22a through Q22j will receive Q25.][1]

Q25. **In the previous question you indicated experiencing a behavior from a service member or civilian working for the military. Please specify in what context this behavior occurred (e.g., during training, with a supervisor present). Please do not include any Personally Identifiable Information (PII) that could identify yourself or others.**

[Participants who responded "Yes" to Q22a, Q22c, Q22d, Q22f, Q22g, Q22h, or Q22i will receive Q26. If a participant responded "No" to all of the listed items, they will skip to the next survey section.]

Q26. **Did any of the behaviors you indicated experiencing from a service member or civilian working for the military include online misconduct (e.g., social media posts, unsolicited contact through the internet)?**

☐ Yes
☐ No

[1] DoD developed and included Question 25 in the survey. As discussed in Chapter Three, DoD should consider removing Question 25 from the final survey.

CHAPTER FIVE

Conclusion

Existing survey efforts do not allow DoD to obtain estimates of hazing or bullying prevalence that align with current DoD definitions of these behaviors. To address this limitation, RAND researchers developed an instrument to estimate the percentage of individuals who experience hazing and bullying each year in the active-duty U.S. military. Before designing this instrument, we first considered whether existing measures could be used to assess the prevalence of hazing and bullying within DoD. After finding that no existing measures were a precise fit to DoD's definitions, we created new, military-specific measures to address the percentage of active-duty service members who experience hazing and bullying each year. In developing this instrument, we sought to create behaviorally based items that align with DoD's definitions of hazing and bullying, which are contained in DoDI 1020.ef. In addition, our DoD sponsor asked that we limit the total number of items to roughly ten to prevent survey fatigue. Therefore, we needed to ensure that the instrument was relatively short.

We first drafted survey items that captured the broad categories of harm described in DoD's definitions of hazing and bullying (DoDI 1020.ef). Then we developed two follow-up items to be answered each time a respondent indicated that he or she had experienced a broad category of behavioral harm. These follow-up items addressed whether each harmful behavioral category that a respondent experienced could be classified as hazing or bullying. After item development, we asked subject-matter experts and DoD experts to review the survey instrument. We modified the instrument based on the comments that we received from these experts (see Appendix B for a revised version of this instrument), and we provided a recommended survey instrument to DoD's OPA for inclusion in a larger survey effort that DoD planned to conduct—namely, the WEOA.

OPA subsequently modified the design of the recommended survey instrument with the goal of facilitating ease of programming (see Appendix C) and to address the context of the assessed behaviors.[1] Compared with the recommended survey instrument, the redesign might increase the cognitive demands placed on participants and increase the risk of biased prevalence estimates due to reading and comprehension errors. Administration and comparison of responses, either in cognitive interviews or in pretests, with the RAND-recommended version of the survey instrument and the OPA-revised version would permit assessment of possible burden and bias. Given time and resource constraints, however, RAND was not asked to assess possibilities of burden or bias. OPA fielded the instrument in 2017 as part of the WEO survey.

RAND researchers conducted cognitive interviewing with a total of 27 participants to assess interpretations of items within the OPA-revised survey instrument. Based on responses from these participants, we modified OPA-revised instrument instructions and items where appropriate. Some participants also commented on the survey structure and OPA-added items. RAND did not modify the survey structure or wording of the OPA-added items, but, to promote clarity, we modified the survey programming associated with the two OPA-added items (see Chapter Four). Administration of the survey instrument contained in Chapter Four will assist DoD in obtaining behaviorally based estimates of the prevalence of hazing and bullying in the active-duty military that align with DoD's definitions of hazing and bullying.

Study Limitations

This effort had several limitations. Because of DoD requirements, the survey instrument developed by RAND was administered to service members within the 2017 WEOA, before cognitive interviewing. Results from the 2017 survey administration could be used to identify potential issues with item structure, wording, skip patterns, and coding. However, the authors

1 No additional details regarding the modifications were available.

did not have access to the 2017 WEOA to assess item performance for this study. In addition, we were not able to conduct comparability analyses to assess similarities and differences in responses to items based on different survey structures. Therefore, we were not able to determine whether the survey structure following expert review and the subsequent OPA revisions were associated with similar or different response patterns.

The cognitive interviewing was conducted with respondents viewing static versions of the questionnaire, rather than a programmed version that skips respondents' past items that are not relevant to their experience. It is likely that the experience of interacting with a personalized version of the survey is different from the experience of viewing a static list of items. In addition, respondents viewed only the hazing and bullying instrument. The WEOA includes additional items, and the influence of those items on the hazing and bullying instrument was not examined.

The survey items focus on bullying and hazing experiences in the past year only. Some service members might have experienced, and could still be affected by, referenced behaviors that occurred more than one year before the day they completed the survey.

Finally, the instrument is intended to assess the prevalence of hazing and bullying among active-duty service members, or the percentage of service members who experienced the behaviors, not the precise number of events each individual experienced. Different categories of referenced behaviors (e.g., "pressure you to consume harmful amounts of alcohol," "hurtfully insult you") might have occurred during the same event. Therefore, the survey instrument cannot identify the number of distinct hazing and bullying events each participant experienced.

APPENDIX A

Summary of Published Hazing and Workplace Bullying and Cyberbullying Survey Instruments

Hazing Measures

National Study of Student Hazing (Allan and Madden, 2008)

The National Study of Student Hazing was conducted by Allan and Madden, 2008, to examine hazing behaviors among students in colleges and universities across the United States. Hazing was defined by the authors as "any activity expected of someone joining or participating in a group that humiliates, degrades, abuses, or endangers them regardless of a person's willingness to participate" (p. 2). The web-based survey used in the study included more than 30 items focused on experiences with hazing behaviors. Students were asked to identify the activities or teams with which they had been most involved in college and then were asked whether various hazing behaviors had happened to them or others as part of joining or belonging to a team or organization. Example items included "be awakened at night by other members" and "be tied up, taped, or confined to small spaces." Response options and psychometric properties of the instrument were not reported. A shorter version of the list of items was used in a study by Norrbom, 2014, of undergraduate students who were members of ethnic Greek-letter organizations. However, the full version of the survey does not appear to have been used elsewhere. In Google Scholar, the study has been cited 114 times.

Questionnaire to Investigate Hazing Among Undergraduate Students (Campo, Poulos, and Sipple, 2005)

Campo, Poulos, and Sipple, 2005, developed a web-based questionnaire to examine hazing among undergraduate students. The questionnaire assessed attitudes, behaviors, and beliefs about hazing among this population. The authors defined hazing as "any activity, required implicitly or explicitly as a condition of initiation or continued membership in an organization, that may negatively impact the physical or psychological well-being of the individual or may cause damage to others, or to public or private property" (p. 137). Nine items within the questionnaire focused on hazing activities that met the university's definition of hazing. Example items include "destroying or stealing property" and "being hit, kicked or physically assaulted in some form." Six additional items focused on "other negative team-building and initiation activities." Examples include "carrying around unnecessary objects or items" and "having food thrown at you or other new members." Respondents were asked about their participation in each of the activities as undergraduate students. Specific response options and the psychometric properties of the questionnaire were not reported. The questionnaire has not been used outside of the original study, although a similar version of the items was adapted for use by Waldron, 2015, among high school and college athletes. In Google Scholar, the study has been cited 105 times.

Questionnaire to Assess Hazing in College Marching Bands (Silveira and Hudson, 2015)

In a study by Silveira and Hudson, 2015, the authors used an online questionnaire to examine hazing in college marching bands. Hazing was defined by the authors as "any activity expected of someone joining a group that humiliates, degrades, abuses, or endangers, regardless of the person's willingness to participate" (p. 12). The questionnaire assessed several aspects of hazing, including students' experiences with hazing behaviors, to whom behaviors are reported, attitudes toward hazing, and awareness of institutional hazing policies. The questionnaire section that focused on experiences with hazing behaviors was composed of a list of 23 hazing behaviors, and respondents were asked about the frequency with which they had experienced each of the behaviors in their college marching band. Participants were asked, "How often have others forced you to do the following?" Example items included "participate in a drinking game" and "deprive yourself of sleep." Response options were "never," "rarely," "sometimes," "often," and "very often." The content validity of the measure was determined based on the level of agreement between two experts who categorized items into themes. For items pertaining to experiences with hazing, high interrater reliability was demonstrated ($\kappa = 0.87$). The questionnaire has not been used outside of this study. In Google Scholar, the study has been cited ten times.

Initiation Survey to Examine Hazing Among Athletes (Waldron, 2015)

Waldron, 2015, defined hazing as "any degrading or abusive behavior required to be socially accepted on a sports team" (p. 1089). The author developed an online survey to analyze the impact of competitive level (high school or college), gender, athletic identity, sport type, and team norms on participation in hazing and positive initiation rituals. An initiation questionnaire within the instrument included nine items assessing severe hazing acts, six items assessing mild hazing acts, and six items assessing positive initiation rituals. Examples of severe hazing activities were "acting as a personal servant to others" and "making body alterations (branding, tattooing, piercing)." Examples of mild hazing activities included "being yelled, cursed, or sworn at" and "being required to remain silent or being silenced." These items aligned with those from Campo, Poulos, and Sipple, 2005, except for one item: "having food thrown at you." Respondents were asked to "list the number of times during the season they participated in each activity as part of team building and initiation while on this sport team" (Waldron, 2015, pp. 1093–1094). The psychometric properties of the initiation questionnaire are not reported. Additionally, the exact questionnaire has not been used outside of this study, although, as mentioned previously, a similar version of the items was originally used by Campo, Poulos, and Sipple, 2005, among undergraduate students. In Google Scholar, the study has been cited four times.

Survey of Hazing Among Fourth-Class Midshipmen and Cadets (GAO, 1992)

A 1990 GAO survey focused on treatment of fourth-class midshipmen and cadets at the Naval Academy, the Air Force Academy, and the Military Academy. Twenty-one items within the broader survey of student treatment focused on hazing. The GAO report highlights the fourth-class indoctrination instruction in effect between 1989 and 1990, which defined hazing as "any unauthorized assumption of authority by a midshipman whereby another midshipman suffers or is exposed to any cruelty, indignity, undue humiliation, hardship, or oppression, or the deprivation or abridgement of any right" (GAO, 1992, p. 13). Example survey items include "had an upperclassman scream in face" and "had to endure verbal harassment, insult, or ridicule." Respondents were asked about the frequency with which they experienced each type of hazing during their fourth-class year, and response options were "never," "one or two times a year," "a couple times a semester," "a couple times a month," "a couple times a week," and "daily or almost daily" (Pershing, 2006). A scale was developed as a measure of the extent of hazing experiences, which totaled responses of cadets and midshipmen across the various types of treatment. The scale's reliability was assessed using Cronbach's coefficient α, ranging from 0.84 to 0.87. The survey does not appear to have been used again, and, according to Google Scholar, the report has never been cited. It was included in this list because of the survey's focus on hazing experiences in a military population.

Workplace Bullying and Cyberbullying Measures

Leymann Inventory of Psychological Terrorization (Leymann, 1990)

Leymann, 1990, defined "psychical terror or mobbing in working life" as "hostile and unethical communication which is directed in a systematic way by one or a number of persons mainly toward one individual" (p. 120). The

LIPT was developed by Leymann to "establish the mobbing frequency in an organization" (p. 120).[1] Originally developed in Swedish, a modified version of the questionnaire, the LIPT-II, has also been adapted into German (Niedl, 1995; Zapf, Knorz, and Kulla, 1996). The instrument contains 45 (LIPT) or 46 (LIPT-II) items, which cover various bullying behaviors (e.g., attacking an individual's relationships and social reputation). Items are scored based on frequency of occurrence, and the scales used have ranged from 3- to 6-point scales. Zapf, Knorz, and Kulla, 1996, identified seven factors through factor analysis and determined the reliability of the scales for two samples to be "attacks with organizational measures (0.79, 0.86), social isolation (0.84, 0.83), attacking private life (0.73, 0.75), physical violence (0.40, 0.69), attacking attitudes (0.52, 0.63), verbal aggression (0.57, 0.66), and rumors (0.71, 0.65)" (Cowie et al., 2002, p. 39). In addition to being used among Swedish and German populations, forms of the LIPT have been translated into other languages and used among other groups, including civil servants in Japan (Tsuno et al., 2010) and employees in southeastern France (Niedhammer, David, and Degioanni, 2006). In Google Scholar, Leymann, 1990, has been cited 1,615 times.

Work Harassment Scale (Björkqvist, Österman, and Hjelt-Bäck, 1992)

The WHS was developed by Björkqvist, Österman, and Hjelt-Bäck to assess harassment between employees. The authors defined harassment as "repeated activities, with the aim of bringing mental (but sometimes also physical) pain, and directed toward one or more individuals who, for one reason or another, are not able to defend themselves" (1994, p. 173). The 24-item WHS questionnaire, which examines a range of work harassment behaviors, excluding sexual harassment, asks respondents how often they feel they have been exposed to various types of "degrading and oppressing activities by their colleagues" during the last six months. Example items

[1] Leymann, 1990, was the original article in which the NAQ was proposed. However, it did not provide detailed information on the measure and its psychometrics. Therefore, Cowie et al., 2002, was reviewed in summarizing this measure. Cowie et al., 2002, did not report examples of items or the response options.

include "sensitive details of your private life used as pressure" and "exposure to direct threats." A 5-point response scale had the following options: 0 = never, 1 = seldom, 2 = occasionally, 3 = often, and 4 = very often. The WHS demonstrated high reliability (Cronbach's α = 0.95). Additionally, a factor analysis of the questionnaire resulted in two subscales of covert aggression: "rational-appearing aggression" and "social manipulation." Rational-appearing aggression included items such as "reduced opportunities to express oneself" and "being interrupted" (Cronbach's α = 0.70). Social manipulation included items such as "spreading of false rumors" and "not being spoken to" (Cronbach's α = 0.82). The questionnaire has been used among other populations, including secondary school teachers in Lithuania (Astrauskaitė, Perminas, and Kern, 2010) and university employees in Finland (Björkqvist, Österman, and Hjelt-Bäck, 1994; Björkqvist, Österman, and Lagerspetz, 1994). In Google Scholar, Björkqvist, Österman, and Hjelt-Bäck, 1994, has been cited 987 times.[2]

Negative Acts Questionnaire (Einarsen and Raknes, 1997)

The NAQ was developed by Einarsen and Raknes, 1997, to study harassment in the workplace. The instrument contains 22 items and measures the frequency with which a respondent has experienced negative acts and harassing behaviors during the past six months. A 5-point scale was used for the response options. The authors identified three primary factors and assessed the reliability of the subscales: personal derogation (Cronbach's α = 0.85), work-related harassment (Cronbach's α = 0.57), and social exclusion (Cronbach's α = 0.33). Two items on social control and one item on physical abuse were also included. Validity of the measure was demonstrated based on strong correlations between self-reported scores on the NAQ and the work environment. The NAQ has been used among other populations, including American workers (Lutgen-Sandvik, Tracy, and Alberts, 2007)

[2] Although Björkqvist, Österman, and Hjelt-Bäck, 1994, is not the original article in which the measure was proposed, this article was used to assess the number of times cited, as Björkqvist, Österman, and Hjelt-Bäck, 1992, and citation information for that article were not available in Google Scholar. Björkqvist, Österman, and Hjelt-Bäck, 1994; Björkqvist, Österman, and Lagerspetz, 1994; and Cowie et al., 2002, were reviewed in summarizing this measure.

and Norwegian victims of bullying (Matthiesen and Einarsen, 2001). In Google Scholar, the study has been cited 943 times.[3]

Negative Acts Questionnaire—Revised (Einarsen, Hoel, and Notelaers, 2009)

The NAQ-R was developed by Einarsen, Hoel, and Notelaers, 2009, to assess exposure to bullying in the workplace. Workplace bullying was defined by the authors as "the persistent exposure to interpersonal aggression and mistreatment from colleagues, superiors or subordinates" (p. 24). The 22-item NAQ-R focuses on bullying experiences in the past six months and encompasses items that fall under work-related bullying, person-related bullying, and physically intimidating bullying. Example items include "being given tasks with unreasonable deadlines" and "repeated reminders of your errors or mistakes." Response options were "never," "now and then," "monthly," "weekly," and "daily." The NAQ-R was shown to be a reliable instrument with high internal consistency, demonstrated by a Cronbach's α of 0.90 for the 22 items. In addition, criterion validity was demonstrated based on a strong Pearson's product-moment correlation between the total score on the NAQ-R and labeling oneself as a bullying victim ($r = 0.54$, $p < 0.001$). Construct validity was also shown based on expected correlations between the NAQ-R and measures of mental health, leadership, and psychosocial work environment. The instrument has been used among other populations, such as nurses (Johnson and Rea, 2009) and athletic trainers (Weuve et al., 2014). In Google Scholar, the study has been cited 678 times.

Generalized Workplace Harassment Questionnaire (Richman et al., 1999)

In their study of university employees, Richman et al., 1999, developed the GWHQ to assess experiences of harassment at work. The 29-item questionnaire evaluates five types of abuse: verbal aggression, disrespectful behavior,

[3] Einarsen and Raknes, 1997, was the original article in which the NAQ was proposed. However, that article was not accessible. Therefore, Cowie et al., 2002, was reviewed in summarizing this measure. Cowie et al., 2002, did not report examples of items or the response options.

isolation/exclusion, threats/bribes, and physical aggression. According to the authors (p. 359),

> Verbal aggression (nine items) consists of hostile verbal exchanges involving yelling or swearing. Disrespectful behavior (nine items) encompasses demeaning experiences such as being humiliated publicly or being talked down to. Isolation/exclusion (five items) involves having one's work contributions ignored or being excluded from important work activities. Threats or bribes (three items) encompass subtle or obvious bribes to do things deemed wrong or threats of retaliation for failing to do such things. Physical aggression (three items) involves being hit, pushed, or grabbed.

Individuals respond by rating each experience as occurring "never," "once," or "more than once in their current job during the past year." Alpha values for the subscales ranged from 0.39 to 0.92. The GWHQ has also been used among nurse educators in the academic workplace (Moss, 2014) and employees in the information technology sector (Low, 2012). Additionally, modified versions of the GWHQ have been used among a national sample of employed adults (Shannon, Rospenda, and Richman, 2007) and among college students in the Midwest (McGinley et al., 2015; Rospenda, Fujishiro, et al., 2017; Rospenda, Richman, et al., 2013). In Google Scholar, the study has been cited 266 times.

Mobbing Scale for Academic Nurses (Ozturk et al., 2008)

Ozturk et al., 2008, defines mobbing as "emotional assaults at workplaces." The Mobbing Scale for Academic Nurses was developed by Ozturk and colleagues to investigate experiences of mobbing among academic nurses. The scale, composed of 60 items, asks respondents to rate the degree to which they agree with statements concerning management attitudes toward mobbing, mobbing behaviors, and effects on victims. Example items include "my professional qualifications are criticized" and "I think that I suffer from psychological and physical distress." A 5-point Likert scale is used for the response options, where 1 = totally disagree and 5 = completely agree. The reliability of the scale was measured through Cronbach's α, which was determined to be 0.97. A factor analysis revealed the following factors:

effects on psychology and fatigue, effects on the organization and management, attacks toward self-esteem, attacks toward personal and professional relationships, effects on social relationships, attacks toward showing oneself and communications, attacks toward professional practices, and effects on health and life. To our knowledge, the questionnaire has not been used outside of the original study, and, in Google Scholar, the study has been cited 56 times.

Cyberbullying Questionnaire–Victim (Gibb and Devereux, 2014)

In their study on cyberbullying behaviors among college students, Gibb and Devereux, 2014, developed a modified version of the Cyberbullying Questionnaire by Calvete et al., 2010, focused on experiences of cyberbullying from the perspective of the victim. The 16-item Cyberbullying Questionnaire–Victim includes items such as "I have had links of humiliating images sent to other people for them to see" and "Someone has recorded video or took pictures by cell phone of me while a group laughed and forced me to do something humiliating or ridiculous." Response options were the following: "never," "within my time at the university," "within the past 3 months," "within the past month," and "within the past week." The Cronbach's α for the scale was 0.94. The measure does not appear to have been used outside of the original study, and, in Google Scholar, the study has been cited 26 times.

Hospital Aggressive Behaviour Scale–Version Co-Workers-Superiors (Waschgler et al., 2013)

The HABS-CS was developed by Waschgler and et al., 2013, to examine lateral and vertical workplace bullying behaviors among nursing staff. Lateral workplace bullying involves hostile behaviors by colleagues, while vertical workplace bullying involves hostile behaviors by superiors. The instrument is composed of 17 items grouped into five factors: (1) active workplace bullying—superior, (2) person-related bullying—colleagues, (3) passive workplace bullying—colleagues, (4) passive workplace bullying—superior, and (5) work-related bullying—colleagues. Example items include "My superior threatens to attack me" under factor 1 and "Some co-workers have stopped talking to me" under factor 3. Response options for the items were not described. The HABS-CS demonstrated high internal consistency (Cronbach's $\alpha = 0.86$). Criterion validity was demonstrated through significant correlations between the factors of the HABS-CS and job satisfaction, burnout components, and psychological well-being. The instrument has not been used outside of the original study, and, in Google Scholar, the study has been cited 16 times.

Workplace Cyberbullying Measure (Farley et al., 2016)

The WCM was developed by Farley et al., 2016, to assess cyberbullying across various work settings. Workplace cyberbullying was defined by the authors as "a situation where over time, an individual is repeatedly subjected to perceived negative acts conducted through technology (e.g. phone, email, websites, and social media) which are related to their work context. In this situation, the target of workplace cyberbullying has difficulty defending him or herself against these actions" (p. 295). The 17-item WCM asks respondents how often over the past six months they had experienced each cyberbullying item through technology in the context of their work. Example items include "received messages that have a disrespectful tone" and "had personal information shared without your permission." Response options were "never," "now and then," "at least monthly," "at least weekly," and "daily." The two factors of the WCM, "work-related cyberbullying" and "person-related cyberbullying," formed two scales, which demonstrated good internal consistencies (work-related, $\alpha = 0.90$; person-related, $\alpha = 0.81$). Additionally, the factors showed convergent factorial validity (work-related factor = 0.90; person-related factor = 0.82). The WCM also showed adequate construct and content validity. The measure has not been used outside of the original study. In Google Scholar, the study has been cited two times.

APPENDIX B

RAND Draft Bullying and Hazing Instrument

This appendix contains the item wording and structure for the hazing and bullying instrument that the RAND team suggests DoD consider implementing, following cognitive pretesting and pilot testing of this instrument. The original version of the instrument was developed before the cognitive interviews being conducted. Postinterview wording refinements, which are described in Chapter Three, have subsequently been incorporated into the instrument listed in this appendix. Throughout the appendix, basic programming notes are in blue; variable labels and coding values are in red; and X date should be set to the month, day, and year that is one year before the date on which the person began the survey.

Instrument Structure Following Expert Review

Instrument Instructions

Sometimes serving in the military involves unpleasant experiences. Some of these are an unavoidable part of official military training or duties. Other unpleasant experiences result from mistreatment that serves no official military purpose. In this section, we ask about unpleasant experiences that served no official military purpose.

When a question mentions a "service member," please include military members of the Active and Reserve Components. They could be at your installation or another installation. They could be acting alone or in coordination with others.

These experiences may have occurred on-duty or off-duty, on-base or off-base, in person or online. Please include them as long as they involved a service member or civilian working for the military.

Instrument

The following questions ask about things that happened within the past 12 months. When you are answering these questions, please do NOT include any events that occurred before [X date].

S1. Since [X date], did a service member or civilian working for the military **threaten or deliberately cause you physical pain** for reasons other than your official military training or duties? For example, they pinned insignia into your skin, hit, kicked, pushed, or slapped you.

Yes 1
No 2

[If a participant responds "Yes" to S1, they will receive the text below and Questions S1a and S1b. If they respond "No" or skip the question without answering, they will skip to Question S2.]

[The following introductory language and both follow-up items should appear together on the same screen.]

You indicated that a service member or civilian working for the military **threatened or deliberately caused you physical pain** for reasons other than your official military training or duties.

S1a. Since [X date], on how many days did this happen to you?

1 day 1
2 days 2
3–9 days 3
10–30 days 4
More than 30 days 5

S1b. Since [X date], was this ever done as part of a tradition, ceremony, or joining a group? For example, it could involve a promotion ceremony, being accepted by coworkers, or starting a new job.

Yes 1
No 2

S2. Since [X date], did a service member or civilian working for the military **deprive you of food, water, or sleep** for reasons other than your official military training or duties?

Yes 1
No 2

[If a participant responds "Yes" to S2, they will receive the text below and Questions S2a and S2b. If they respond "No" or skip the question without answering, they will skip to S3.]

[The following introductory language and both follow-up items should appear together on the same screen.]

You indicated a service member or civilian working for the military **deprived you of food, water, or sleep** for reasons other than your official military training or duties.

S2a. Since [X date], on how many days did this happen to you?

1 day 1
2 days 2
3–9 days 3
10–30 days 4
More than 30 days 5

S2b. Since [X date], was this ever done as part of a tradition, ceremony, or joining a group? For example, it could involve a promotion ceremony, being accepted by coworkers, or starting a new job.

Yes 1
No 2

S3. Since [X date], did a service member or civilian working for the military **pressure you to consume harmful amounts of alcohol, water, or other substances** for reasons other than your official military training or duties?

Yes 1
No 2

[If a participant responds "Yes" to S3, they will receive the text below and Questions S3a and S3b. If they respond "No" or skip the question without answering, they will skip to Question S4.]

[The following introductory language and both follow-up items should appear together on the same screen.]

You indicated a service member or civilian working for the military **pressured you to consume harmful amounts of alcohol, water, or other substances** for reasons other than your official military training or duties.

S3a. Since [X date], on how many days did this happen to you?

1 day 1
2 days 2
3–9 days 3
10–30 days 4
More than 30 days 5

S3b. Since [X date], was this ever done as part of a tradition, ceremony, or joining a group? For example, it could involve a promotion ceremony, being accepted by coworkers, or starting a new job.

Yes 1
No 2

S4. Since [X date], did a service member or civilian working for the military **subject you to a cruel prank or abuse you** for reasons other than your official military training or duties? For example, they intentionally left you stranded, or bound, taped, shaved, or painted your body.

Yes 1
No 2

[If a participant responds "Yes" to S4, they will receive the text below and Questions S4a and S4b. If they respond "No" or skip the question without answering, they will skip to S5.]

[The following introductory language and both follow-up items should appear together on the same screen.]

You indicated a service member or civilian working for the military **subjected you to a cruel prank or abused you** for reasons other than your official military training or duties.

S4a. Since [X date], on how many days did this happen to you?

1 day 1
2 days 2
3–9 days 3
10–30 days 4
More than 30 days 5

S4b. Since [X date], was this ever done as part of a tradition, ceremony, or joining a group? For example, it could involve a promotion ceremony, being accepted by coworkers, or starting a new job.

Yes 1
No 2

S5. Since [X date], did a service member or civilian working for the military **take or damage your property** for reasons other than your official military training or duties?

Yes 1
No 2

[If a participant responds "Yes" to S5, they will receive the text below and Questions S5a and S5b. If they respond "No" or skip the question without answering, they will skip to S6.]

[The following introductory language and both follow-up items should appear together on the same screen.]

You indicated a service member or civilian working for the military **took or damaged your property** for reasons other than your official military training or duties.

S5a. Since [X date], on how many days did this happen to you?

1 day 1
2 days 2
3–9 days 3
10–30 days 4
More than 30 days 5

S5b. Since [X date], was this ever done as part of a tradition, ceremony, or joining a group? For example, it could involve a promotion ceremony, being accepted by coworkers, or starting a new job.

Yes 1
No 2

S6. Since [X date], did a service member or civilian working for the military **pressure you to do something illegal or dangerous** for reasons other than your official military training or duties? For example, they pressured you to take risks to prove your bravery, steal something, or harm another person.

Yes 1
No 2

[If a participant responds "Yes" to S6, they will receive the text below and Questions S6a and S6b. If they respond "No" or skip the question without answering, they will skip to Question S7.]

[The following introductory language and both follow-up items should appear together on the same screen.]

You indicated a service member or civilian working for the military **pressured you to do something illegal or dangerous** for reasons other than your official military training or duties.

S6a. Since [X date], on how many days did this happen to you?

1 day 1
2 days 2
3–9 days 3
10–30 days 4
More than 30 days 5

S6b. Since [X date], was this ever done as part of a tradition, ceremony, or joining a group? For example, it could involve a promotion ceremony, being accepted by coworkers, or starting a new job.

Yes 1
No 2

S7. Since [X date], did a service member or civilian working for the military **try to humiliate you** for reasons other than your official military training or duties? For example, they shared nude pictures without your permission, spread hurtful gossip about you, or made you do something embarrassing.

Yes 1
No 2

[If a participant responds "Yes" to S7, they will receive the text below and Questions S7a and S7b. If they respond "No" or skip the question without answering, they will skip to Question S8.]

[The following introductory language and both follow-up items should appear together on the same screen.]

You indicated a service member or civilian working for the military **tried to humiliate you** for reasons other than your official military training or duties.

S7a. Since [X date], on how many days did this happen to you?

1 day 1
2 days 2
3–9 days 3
10–30 days 4
More than 30 days 5

S7b. Since [X date], was this ever done as part of a tradition, ceremony, or joining a group? For example, it could involve a promotion ceremony, being accepted by coworkers, or starting a new job.

Yes 1
No 2

S8. Since [X date], did a service member or civilian working for the military **hurtfully insult you** for reasons other than your official military training or duties? For example, they made fun of your appearance or tried to upset you by calling you a fag or retard.

Yes 1
No 2

[If a participant responds "Yes" to S8, they will receive the text below and Questions S8a and S8b. If they respond "No" or skip the question without answering, they will skip to Question S9.]

[The following introductory language and both follow-up items should appear together on the same screen.]

You indicated a service member or civilian working for the military **hurtfully insulted you** for reasons other than your official military training or duties.

S8a. Since [X date], on how many days did this happen to you?

1 day 1
2 days 2
3–9 days 3
10–30 days 4
More than 30 days 5

S8b. Since [X date], was this ever done as part of a tradition, ceremony, or joining a group? For example, it could involve a promotion ceremony, being accepted by coworkers, or starting a new job.

Yes 1
No 2

S9. Since [X date], did a service member or civilian working for the military **pressure you to engage in disgusting activities** for reasons other than your official military training or duties? For example, put something gross in your mouth, threw you in unsanitary water, or encouraged you to urinate on someone.

Yes 1
No 2

[If a participant responds "Yes" to S9, they will receive the text below and Questions S9a and S9b. If they respond "No" or skip the question without answering, they will skip to Question S10.]

[The following introductory language and both follow-up items should appear together on the same screen.]

You indicated a service member or civilian working for the military **pressured you to engage in disgusting activities** for reasons other than your official military training or duties.

S9a. Since [X date], on how many days did this happen to you?

1 day 1
2 days 2
3–9 days 3
10–30 days 4
More than 30 days 5

S9b. Since [X date], was this ever done as part of a tradition, ceremony, or joining a group? For example, it could involve a promotion ceremony, being accepted by coworkers, or starting a new job.

Yes 1
No 2

S10. Since [X date], did a service member or civilian working for the military **touch your private body parts, or make you touch theirs, when they knew this contact was unwanted** for reasons other than your official military training or duties? For example, they pressed their crotch on you, put something in your rectum, or groped you.

Yes 1
No 2

[If a participant responds "Yes" to S10, they will receive the text below and Questions S10a and S10b. If they respond "No" to or skip the question without answering, they will skip to the next survey section.]

You indicated a service member or civilian working for the military **touched your private body parts, or made you touch theirs, when they knew this contact was unwanted** for reasons other than your official military training or duties.

[The following introductory language and both follow-up items should appear together on the same screen.]

S10a. Since [X date], on how many days did this happen to you?

1 day 1
2 days 2
3–9 days 3
10–30 days 4
More than 30 days 5

S10b. Since [X date], was this ever done as part of a tradition, ceremony, or joining a group? For example, it could involve a promotion ceremony, being accepted by coworkers, or starting a new job.

Yes 1
No 2

APPENDIX C

Department of Defense–Revised Bullying and Hazing Instrument

As discussed in Chapter One, DoD restructured the instrument with the goal of facilitating ease of programming, and, during this restructure, DoD added two survey items (Question 26 and Question 27 in this appendix). RAND researchers used the DoD-restructured instrument design, listed in this appendix, in cognitive interviews. We were not tasked with comparing participants' reactions to each instrument design, but we were able to gather information about the restructured instrument during cognitive interviews. This appendix contains an assessment of how survey participants might respond differently to survey items on the RAND and DoD-restructured instruments—information that was provided to DoD before initiation of cognitive interviews. The primary differences between the initial survey design and the subsequent DoD-restructured design included elimination of the repetition of the item stem indicating the time frame and restructuring of follow-up survey items into tables, rather than placement of relevant items immediately after each screening item. Since Appendix B contains the survey format that RAND recommends, the wording changes that are described in Chapter Three have been incorporated into Appendix B, but we have not incorporated those changes into this appendix.

Compared with the original instrument design, the DoD-restructured instrument might require less time of participants, as they do not have to read "Since [X date], did a military employee . . ." as part of each item.

However, rereading this reminder in each item might be important to ensure that participants indicate experiences that occurred in the past year only. In the DoD-restructured table formats, participants might be more likely to initially skip the item stem or forget the time frame as they work through the survey questions. Responses outside the desired time frame could bias prevalence estimates upward if some participants begin providing responses for their lifetime or career experiences, rather than limiting themselves to the past year.

For the DoD-restructured survey item tables addressing hazing and bullying (Questions 24 and 25), the table format might require more time of participants than that of the initial instrument design. In the DoD-restructured format, participants need to read each behavior three times—once before answering the experience question (Question 22), a second time before answering the hazing question (Question 24), and a third time before answering the bullying question (Question 25). For a hypothetical participant who had experienced every hazing/bullying behavior, the table format in Questions 24 and 25 would require reading more words than the instrument design following expert review. That is, in the DoD-restructured table format, the savings from not repeating the stem are eliminated by repeating the behaviors.

In addition to the number of words, the DoD-restructured table format might increase cognitive load for the follow-up questions (Questions 24 and 25). Participants need to orient to the specified behavior for each question. This cognitive load is likely reduced in the instrument design format created following expert review (Goldstein, 2014), in which the participant orients to the behavior a single time and then answers the follow-up questions in succession.

Further, many survey takers either skip or skim table stems. If a participant does not read the stems to Questions 24 and 25, it might look like the original screening questions are being repeated a second time. Therefore, some participants might see what looks like the same items again and become frustrated, leading to potential dropout.

Hazing/Bullying Instrument (Subset of the Workplace and Equal Opportunity Survey)

The following questions ask about things that happened within the past 12 months. For these items, "military member" may refer to anyone in your chain of command, including DoD civilians. When you are answering these questions, please do NOT include any events that occurred before [Date that is 12 months before today's date will be inserted throughout; X date].

Q22. **Since** [date exactly one year ago; X date]**, did a military member**[1] **. . .**
Mark "Yes" or "No" for each item.

	Yes	No
Q22a. **Threaten or deliberately cause you physical pain** for reasons other than your official military training or duties? For example, they pinned insignia into your skin, or hit, kicked, pushed, or slapped you.	1 ☐	2 ☐
Q22b. **Deprive you of food, water, or sleep** for reasons other than your official military training or duties?	1 ☐	2 ☐
Q22c. **Pressure you to consume harmful amounts of alcohol, water, or other substances** for reasons other than your official military training or duties?	1 ☐	2 ☐
Q22d. **Harmfully trick or abuse you for reasons other than your official military training or duties?** For example, they intentionally left you stranded, or bound, taped, shaved, or painted your body.	1 ☐	2 ☐
Q22e. **Take or damage your property** for reasons other than your official military training or duties?	1 ☐	2 ☐
Q22f. **Pressure you to do something illegal or dangerous** for reasons other than your official military training or duties? For example, they pressured you to take risks to prove your bravery, steal something, or harm another person.	1 ☐	2 ☐
Q22g. **Try to humiliate you** for reasons other than your official military training or duties? For example, they shared nude pictures without your permission, spread hurtful gossip about you online, or made you pretend to have sex.	1 ☐	2 ☐
Q22h. **Hurtfully insult you** for reasons other than your official military training or duties? For example, they made fun of your appearance or tried to upset you by calling you a fag or dyke.	1 ☐	2 ☐
Q22i. **Pressure you to engage in disgusting activities** for reasons other than your official military training or duties? For example, put something gross in your mouth, threw you in unsanitary water, or encouraged you to urinate on someone.	1 ☐	2 ☐
Q22j. **Touch your private body parts, or make you touch theirs, when they knew this contact was unwanted?** For example, they pressed their crotch on you, put something in your rectum, or groped you.	1 ☐	2 ☐

[1] Based on cognitive interviews with service members, we recommend that "military member" be revised to "service member or civilian working for the military."

[If a participant responds "Yes" to Q22j, they will receive Q23. If they respond "No" to or skip the question without answering, they will skip to the next survey section.]

Q23. [This question is asked only if the person answered "yes" to "j" above] **You indicated a military member touched your private body parts, or made you touch his/hers, when he/she knew this contact was unwanted. Was this part of an official medical exam or for another official military purpose?**

☐ Yes 1

☐ No 2

[Participants who responded "No" to all items in Q22 will skip Q23, all items in Q24, and all items in Q25, Q26, and Q27. After completing items Q22a through Q22j, participants who responded "Yes" to any one of the items in Q22a through Q22i will receive the corresponding items in Q24. If they respond "No" to an item in Q22a through Q22i, they will not receive the corresponding item in Q24. For example, if a participant responds "Yes" to Q22a, they will receive Q24a. If they respond "No" to Q22a, they will not receive Q24a. If a participant responds "Yes" to Q22j and "No" to Q23, they will receive Q24j. If they respond "Yes" to Q22j and "Yes" to Q23, they will not receive Q24j.]

You indicated in the previous questions that within the past 12 months you experienced behaviors from a military member. The following questions ask about the purpose of the misconduct.

Q24. [If a question from Q22 is answered "yes," a corresponding follow-up question will be asked next. People who answered "no" will not see the follow-up question.] **Since** [date exactly one year ago; X date]**, was this misconduct ever done as part of a tradition, ceremony, or joining a group? For example, it could involve a promotion ceremony, being accepted by coworkers, or starting a new job.** ***Mark "Yes" or "No" for each item.***

	Yes	No
Q24a. A military member **threatened or deliberately caused you physical pain** for reasons other than your official military training or duties? For example, they pinned insignia into your skin, or hit, kicked, pushed, or slapped you.	1 ☐	2 ☐
Q24b. A military member **deprived you of food, water, or sleep** for reasons other than your official military training or duties?	1 ☐	2 ☐
Q24c. A military member **pressured you to consume harmful amounts of alcohol, water, or other substances** for reasons other than your official military training or duties?	1 ☐	2 ☐
Q24d. A military member **harmfully tricked or abused you for reasons other than your official military training or duties?** For example, he/she intentionally left you stranded, or bound, taped, shaved, or painted your body.	1 ☐	2 ☐
Q24e. A military member **took or damaged your property** for reasons other than your official military training or duties?	1 ☐	2 ☐
Q24f. A military member **pressured you to do something illegal or dangerous** for reasons other than your official military training or duties? For example, he/she pressured you to take risks to prove your bravery, steal something, or harm another person.	1 ☐	2 ☐
Q24g. A military member **tried to humiliate you** for reasons other than your official military training or duties? For example, he/she shared nude pictures without your permission, spread hurtful gossip about you online, or made you pretend to have sex.	1 ☐	2 ☐
Q24h. A military member **hurtfully insulted you** for reasons other than your official military training or duties? For example, he/she made fun of your appearance or tried to upset you by calling you a fag or dyke.	1 ☐	2 ☐
Q24i. A military member **pressured you to engage in disgusting activities** for reasons other than your official military training or duties? For example, put something gross in your mouth, threw you in unsanitary water, or encouraged you to urinate on someone.	1 ☐	2 ☐
Q24j. A military member **touched your private body parts, or made you touch his/hers,** when he/she knew this contact was unwanted, and it was not part of an official medical exam or other official military purpose.	1 ☐	2 ☐

[After completing Q24, participants who responded "Yes" to any one of the items in Q22a through Q22i will receive the corresponding items in Q25. If they respond "No" to an item in Q22a through Q22i, they will not receive the corresponding item in Q25. For example, if a participant responds "Yes" to Q22a, they will receive Q25a. If they respond "No" to Q22a, they will not receive Q25a. If a participant responds "Yes" to Q22j and "No" to Q23, they will receive Q25j. If they respond "Yes" to Q22j and "Yes" to Q23, they will not receive Q25j.]

You indicated in the previous questions that within the past 12 months you experienced behaviors from a military member. The following questions ask about the frequency that these behaviors occurred.

Q25. [If a question from 22 is answered "yes," a corresponding follow-up question will be asked next. People who answered "no" will not see the follow-up question.] **Since** [date exactly one year ago]**, on how many days did this happen to you?** ***Mark one answer for each item.***

	More than 30 days	10–30 days	3–9 days	2 days	1 day
Q25a. A military member **threatened or deliberately caused you physical pain** for reasons other than your official military training or duties? For example, they pinned insignia into your skin, or hit, kicked, pushed, or slapped you.	5 ☐	4 ☐	3 ☐	2 ☐	1 ☐
Q25b. A military member **deprived you of food, water, or sleep** for reasons other than your official military training or duties?	5 ☐	4 ☐	3 ☐	2 ☐	1 ☐
Q25c. A military member **pressured you to consume harmful amounts of alcohol, water, or other substances** for reasons other than your official military training or duties?	5 ☐	4 ☐	3 ☐	2 ☐	1 ☐
Q25d. A military member **harmfully tricked or abused you for reasons other than your official military training or duties?** For example, he/she intentionally left you stranded, or bound, taped, shaved, or painted your body.	5 ☐	4 ☐	3 ☐	2 ☐	1 ☐
Q25e. A military member **took or damaged your property** for reasons other than your official military training or duties?	5 ☐	4 ☐	3 ☐	2 ☐	1 ☐
Q25f. A military member **pressured you to do something illegal or dangerous** for reasons other than your official military training or duties? For example, he/she pressured you to take risks to prove your bravery, steal something, or harm another person.	5 ☐	4 ☐	3 ☐	2 ☐	1 ☐
Q25g. A military member **tried to humiliate you** for reasons other than your official military training or duties? For example, he/she shared nude pictures without your permission, spread hurtful gossip about you online, or made you pretend to have sex.	5 ☐	4 ☐	3 ☐	2 ☐	1 ☐

	More than 30 days	10–30 days	3–9 days	2 days	1 day
Q25h. A military member **hurtfully insulted you** for reasons other than your official military training or duties? For example, he/she made fun of your appearance or tried to upset you by calling you a fag or dyke.	5 ☐	4 ☐	3 ☐	2 ☐	1 ☐
Q25i. A military member **pressured you to engage in disgusting activities** for reasons other than your official military training or duties? For example, put something gross in your mouth, threw you in unsanitary water, or encouraged you to urinate on someone.	5 ☐	4 ☐	3 ☐	2 ☐	1 ☐
Q25j. A military member **touched your private body parts, or make you touch his/hers,** when he/she knew this contact was unwanted, and it was not part of an official medical exam or other official military purpose.	5 ☐	4 ☐	3 ☐	2 ☐	1 ☐

[After completing Q24 and Q25, participants who responded "Yes" to any one of the items in Q22a through Q22i will receive Q26 and Q27. If a participant responds "Yes" to Q22j and "No" to Q23, they will receive Q26 and Q27. If they respond "Yes" to Q22j and "Yes" to Q23, they will not receive Q25j.]

Q26. [This question is asked only if the person answered "Yes" to any question from Q22] **In the previous question you indicated experiencing a behavior from a military member. Please specify in what context this behavior occurred (e.g., during training, with a supervisor present). Please do not include any Personally Identifiable Information (PII) that could identify yourself or others.**

Q27. [This question is asked only if the person answered "Yes" to any question from Q22] **Did any of the behaviors you indicated experiencing from a military member include online misconduct (e.g., social media posts, unsolicited contact through the internet)?**

- ☐ Yes 1
- ☐ No 2

References

Allan, Elizabeth, David Kerschner, and Jessica M. Payne, "College Student Hazing Experiences, Attitudes, and Perceptions: Implications for Prevention," *Journal of Student Affairs, Research, and Practice*, Vol. 56, No. 1, 2019, pp. 32–48.

Allan, Elizabeth J., and Mary Madden, *Hazing in View: College Students at Risk*, Orono, Me.: University of Maine, March 11, 2008.

Alwin, Duane F., and Brett A. Beattie, "The KISS Principle in Survey Design: Question Length and Data Quality," *Sociological Methodology*, Vol. 46, No. 1, 2016, pp. 121–152.

Anusiewicz, Colleen V., Peng Li, and Patricia A. Patrician, "Measuring Workplace Bullying in a U.S. Nursing Population with the Short Negative Acts Questionnaire," *Research in Nursing and Health*, Vol. 44, 2021, pp. 319-328.

Astrauskaitė, Milda, Aidas Perminas, and Roy M. Kern, "Sickness, Colleagues' Harassment in Teachers' Work and Emotional Exhaustion," *Medicina (Kaunas)*, Vol. 46, No. 9, 2010, pp. 628–634.

Björkqvist, Kaj, Karin Österman, and Monika Hjelt-Bäck, "Work Harassment Scale," Vaasa, Finland: Department of Psychology, Abo Akademi University, 1992.

———, "Aggression Among University Employees," *Aggressive Behavior*, Vol. 20, No. 3, 1994, pp. 173–184.

Björkqvist, Kaj, Karin Österman, and Kirsti M. J. Lagerspetz, "Sex Differences in Covert Aggression Among Adults," *Aggressive Behavior*, Vol. 20, No. 1, 1994, pp. 27–33.

Calvete, Esther, Izaskun Orue, Ana Estévez, Lourdes Villardón, and Patricia Padilla, "Cyberbullying in Adolescents: Modalities and Aggressors' Profile," *Computers in Human Behavior*, Vol. 26, No. 5, September 2010, pp. 1128–1135.

Campo, Shelly, Gretchen Poulos, and John W. Sipple, "Prevalence and Profiling: Hazing Among College Students and Points of Intervention," *American Journal of Health Behavior*, Vol. 29, No. 2, 2005, pp. 137–149.

Cohen, William A., "Hazing," memorandum for the Secretaries of the Military Departments et al., Washington, D.C.: U.S. Department of Defense, August 28, 1997.

Cowie, Helen, Paul Naylor, Ian Rivers, Peter K. Smith, and Beatriz Pereira, "Measuring Workplace Bullying," *Aggression and Violent Behavior*, Vol. 7, No. 1, 2002, pp. 33–51.

Defense Manpower Data Center, *2013 Workplace and Equal Opportunity Survey of Active Duty Members: Nonresponse Bias Analysis Report*, Ft. Belvoir, Va.: Defense Technical Information Center, DMDC Report No. 2013-046, 2014.

——, *Status of Forces Surveys of Active Duty Members (2013 & 2014 SOFS-A)*, March 2016. As of September 13, 2018: https://download.militaryonesource.mil/12038/MOS/Reports/SOFS-A_Briefing_20160311.pdf

Einarsen, Staale, Helge Hoel, and Guy Notelaers, "Measuring Exposure to Bullying and Harassment at Work: Validity, Factor Structure and Psychometric Properties of the Negative Acts Questionnaire—Revised," *Work & Stress*, Vol. 23, No. 1, 2009, pp. 24–44.

Einarsen, Ståle, and Bjørn I. Raknes, "Harassment in the Workplace and the Victimization of Men," *Violence and Victims*, Vol. 12, No. 3, February 1997, pp. 247–263.

Escartin, Jordi, Ivana Vranjes, Elfi Baillien, and Guy Notelaers, "Workplace Bullying and Cyberbullying Scales: An Overview," in Premilla D'Cruz, Ernesto Noronha, Guy Notelaers, and Charlotte Rayner, eds., *Concepts, Approaches and Methods*, Handbooks of Workplace Bullying, Emotional Abuse and Harassment, Singapore: Springer, 2019, pp. 1–37.

Farley, Samuel, Iain Coyne, Carolyn Axtell, and Christine Sprigg, "Design, Development and Validation of a Workplace Cyberbullying Measure, the WCM," *Work & Stress*, Vol. 30, No. 4, 2016, pp. 293–317.

Gibb, Zebbedia G., and Paul G. Devereux, "Who Does That Anyway? Predictors and Personality Correlates of Cyberbullying in College," *Computers in Human Behavior*, Vol. 38, 2014, pp. 8–16.

Goldstein, E. Bruce, *Cognitive Psychology: Connecting Mind, Research and Everyday Experience*, Scarborough, Ontario: Nelson Education, 2014.

Goodboy, Alan K., Matthew M. Martin, and San Bolkan, "Workplace Bullying and Work Engagement: A Self-Determination Model," *Journal of Interpersonal Violence*, Vol. 35, No. 2, 2020, pp. 4686–4708.

Johnson, Susan L., and Ruth E. Rea, "Workplace Bullying: Concerns for Nurse Leaders," *Journal of Nursing Administration*, Vol. 39, No. 2, February 2009, pp. 84–90.

Jonsson, Sandra, Tuija Muhonen, Rebecka Cowen Forssell, and Martin Backstrom, "Assessing Exposure to Bullying Through Digital Devices in Working Life: Two Versions of a Cyberbullying Questionnaire (CBQ)," *Psychology*, Vol. 8, 2017, pp. 477–494.

Keller, Kirsten M., Laura L. Miller, Sean Robson, Coreen Farris, Brian D. Stucky, Marian Oshiro, and Sarah O. Meadows, *An Integrated Survey System for Addressing Abuse and Misconduct Toward Air Force Trainees During Basic Military Training*, Santa Monica, Calif.: RAND Corporation, RR-964-AF, 2015. As of September 30, 2019: https://www.rand.org/pubs/research_reports/RR964.html

Lenzer, Timo, Lars Kaczmirek, and Alwine Lenzner, "Cognitive Burden of Survey Questions and Response Times: A Psycholinguistic Experiment," *Applied Cognitive Psychology*, Vol. 24, 2010, pp. 1003–1020.

Leymann, Heinz, "Mobbing and Psychological Terror at Workplaces," *Violence and Victims*, Vol. 5, No. 2, 1990, pp. 119–126.

Low, Sze Zen, *Workplace Harassment and Counterproductive Work Behaviors: A Daily Diary Investigation*, doctoral dissertation, Long Beach, Calif.: California State University, Long Beach, 2012.

Lutgen-Sandvik, Pamela, Sarah J. Tracy, and Jess K. Alberts, "Burned by Bullying in the American Workplace: Prevalence, Perception, Degree and Impact," *Journal of Management Studies*, Vol. 44, No. 6, 2007, pp. 837–862.

Makarem, Nisrine N., Lucy R. Tavitian-Elmadjian, Dayana Brome, Ghassan N. Hamadeh, and Stale Einarsen, "Assessment of Workplace Bullying: Reliability and Validity of an Arabic Version of the Negative Acts Questionnaire-Revised (NAQ-R)," *BMJ Open*, Vol. 8, No. 12, 2018.

Matthiesen, Stig Berge, and Ståle Einarsen, "MMPI-2 Configurations Among Victims of Bullying at Work," *European Journal of Work and Organizational Psychology*, Vol. 10, No. 4, 2001, pp. 467–484.

Mawritz, Mary B., Johnna Capitano, Rebecca L. Greenbaum, Julena M. Bonner, and Joongseo Kim, "Development and Validation of the Workplace Hazing Scale," *Human Relations*, online ahead of print, 2020, pp. 1–38. As of August 24, 2021:
https://doi.org/10.1177/0018726720957058

McGinley, Meredith, Kathleen M. Rospenda, Li Liu, and Judith A. Richman, "Chronic Generalized Harassment During College: Influences on Alcohol and Drug Use," *Journal of Youth and Adolescence*, Vol. 44, No. 10, 2015, pp. 1898–1913.

Miller, Laura L., Coreen Farris, Marek N. Posard, Miriam Matthews, Kirsten M. Keller, Sean Robson, Stephanie Brooks Holliday, Mauri Matsuda, Rachel M. Burns, Lisa Wagner, and Barbara Bicksler, *A Survey System to Assess Abuse and Misconduct Toward Air Force Students in Occupational Specialty Training*, Santa Monica, Calif.: RAND Corporation, RR-2692-AF, 2019. As of September 30, 2019:
https://www.rand.org/pubs/research_reports/RR2692.html

Moss, Kimberly D., *Age-Related Intergenerational Tension, Harassment, Perceived Self-Efficacy, and Job Satisfaction of Nurse Educators in the Academic Workplace*, doctoral dissertation, Minneapolis, Minn.: Capella University, 2014.

Neuman, Joel H., "Aggression, Unethical Behavior, and Employee Well-Being: An 'Aggressive' Examination of the Issues," in Robert A. Giacalone and Mark D. Promislo, eds., *Handbook of Unethical Work Behavior: Implications for Well-Being*, Armonk, N.Y.: M. E. Sharpe, 2013, pp. 89–103.

Neuman, Joel H., and Loraleigh Keashly, "Bullies Coming Out of the Schoolyard and into the Boardroom: Combating Abusive Workplace Communication," in Jason S. Wrench, ed., *Workplace Communication for the 21st Century: Tools and Strategies That Impact the Bottom Line*, Santa Barbara, Calif.: Praeger, 2013, pp. 321–354.

Niedhammer, Isabelle, Simone David, and Stephanie Degioanni, "Association Between Workplace Bullying and Depressive Symptoms in the French Working Population," *Journal of Psychosomatic Research*, Vol. 61, No. 2, August 2006, pp. 251–259.

Niedl, Klaus, *Mobbing/Bullying am Arbeitsplatz* [*Mobbing/Bullying at the Workplace*], München und Mering: Rainer Hampp, 1995.

Norrbom, Melissa Allyn Ann, *A Study of Hazing: Perceptions Within Recently Established Ethnic-Based Greek Letter Organizations*, Sacramento, Calif.: California State University, 2014.

ODMEO—*See* Office of Diversity Management and Equal Opportunity.

Office of Diversity Management and Equal Opportunity, *Hazing Prevention and Response in the Armed Forces: Annual Summary Report to Congress*, Washington D.C.: Department of Defense, 2017.

Office of People Analytics, *2016 Service Academy Gender Relations Survey: Overview Report*, Ft. Belvoir, Va.: Defense Technical Information Center, OPA Report No. 2016-043, 2017.

Office of the Under Secretary of Defense for Personnel and Readiness, *DoD Instruction 1020.03: Harassment Prevention and Response in the Armed Forces*, Washington D.C.: Department of Defense, February 8, 2018.

OPA—*See* Office of People Analytics.

Ozturk, Havva, Serap Sokmen, Fatma Yilmaz, and Dilek Cilingir, "Measuring Mobbing Experiences of Academic Nurses: Development of a Mobbing Scale," *Journal of the American Association of Nurse Practitioners*, Vol. 20, No. 9, 2008, pp. 435–442.

Park, Mijeong, and Jeong Sil Choi, "Effects of Workplace Cyberbullying on Nurses' Symptom Experience and Turnover Intention," *Journal of Nursing Management*, Vol. 27, 2019, pp. 1108–1115.

Pershing, Jana L., "Men and Women's Experiences with Hazing in a Male-Dominated Elite Military Institution," *Men and Masculinities*, Vol. 8, No. 4, 2006, pp. 470–492.

Reid, Gerald M., Melissa K. Holt, Erika D. Felix, and Jennifer Greif Green, "Perceived Consequences of Hazing Exposure During the First Year of College: Associations with Childhood Victimization," *Journal of American College Health*, Vol. 67, No. 5, 2019, pp. 402–409.

Richman, Judith A., Kathleen M. Rospenda, Stephanie J. Nawyn, Joseph A. Flaherty, Michael Fendrich, Melinda L. Drum, and Timothy P. Johnson, "Sexual Harassment and Generalized Workplace Abuse Among University Employees: Prevalence and Mental Health Correlates," *American Journal of Public Health*, Vol. 89, No. 3, March 1999, pp. 358–363.

Rospenda, Kathleen M., Kaori Fujishiro, Meredith McGinley, Jennifer M. Wolff, and Judith A. Richman, "Effects of Workplace Generalized and Sexual Harassment on Abusive Drinking Among First Year Male and Female College Students: Does Prior Drinking Experience Matter?" *Substance Use & Misuse*, Vol. 52, No. 7, 2017, pp. 892–904.

Rospenda, Kathleen M., Judith A. Richman, Jennifer M. Wolff, and Larisa A. Burke, "Bullying Victimization Among College Students: Negative Consequences for Alcohol Use," *Journal of Addictive Diseases*, Vol. 32, No. 4, 2013, pp. 325–342.

Shannon, Candice A., Kathleen M. Rospenda, and Judith A. Richman, "Workplace Harassment Patterning, Gender, and Utilization of Professional Services: Findings from a U.S. National Study," *Social Science & Medicine*, Vol. 64, No. 6, 2007, pp. 1178–1191.

Silveira, Jason M., and Michael W. Hudson, "Hazing in the College Marching Band," *Journal of Research in Music Education*, Vol. 63, No. 1, 2015, pp. 5–27.

Tsuno, Kanami, Norito Kawakami, Akiomi Inoue, and Kiyoko Abe, "Measuring Workplace Bullying: Reliability and Validity of the Japanese Version of the Negative Acts Questionnaire," *Journal of Occupational Health*, Vol. 52, No. 4, 2010, pp. 216–226.

U.S. General Accounting Office (GAO), *DoD Service Academies: More Changes Needed to Eliminate Hazing*, Washington, D.C.: National Security and International Affairs Division, 1992.

Vranjes, Ivana, Elfi Baillien, Heidi Vandebosch, Sara Erreygers, and Hans De Witte, "When Workplace Bullying Goes Online: Construction and Validation of the Inventory of Cyberbullying Acts at Work (ICA-W)," *European Journal of Work and Organizational Psychology*, Vol. 27, No. 1, 2018, pp. 28–39.

Waldron, Jennifer J., "Predictors of Mild Hazing, Severe Hazing, and Positive Initiation Rituals in Sport," *Journal of Sports Science & Coaching*, Vol. 10, No. 6, 2015, pp. 1089–1101.

Waldron, Jennifer J., and Christopher L. Kowalski, "Crossing the Line," *Research Quarterly for Exercise and Sport*, Vol. 80, No. 2, 2009, pp. 291–302.

Waldron, Jennifer J., Quinten Lynn, and Vikki Krane, "Duct Tape, Icy Hot & Paddles: Narrative of Initiation onto U.S. Male Sport Teams," *Sport, Education and Society*, Vol. 16, No. 1, 2011, pp. 111–125.

Waschgler, Kathrin, José Antonio Ruiz-Hernández, Bartolomé Llor-Esteban, and José Antonio Jiménez-Barbero, "Vertical and Lateral Workplace Bullying in Nursing: Development of the Hospital Aggressive Behaviour Scale," *Journal of Interpersonal Violence*, Vol. 28, No. 12, 2013, pp. 2389–2412.

Weuve, Celest, William A. Pitney, Malissa Martin, and Stephanie M. Mazerolle, "Perceptions of Workplace Bullying Among Athletic Trainers in the Collegiate Setting," *Journal of Athletic Training*, Vol. 49, No. 5, 2014, pp. 706–718.

Willis, Gordon, *Cognitive Interviews: A Tool for Improving Questionnaire Design*, Thousand Oaks, Calif.: Sage, 2005.

Work, Robert O., "Hazing and Bullying Prevention and Response in the Armed Forces," memorandum for the Secretaries of the Military Departments et al., Washington D.C.: Deputy Secretary of Defense, December 23, 2015.

Yamada, David C., "Workplace Bullying and American Employment Law: A Ten-Year Progress Report and Assessment," *Comparative Labor Law & Policy Journal*, Vol. 32, No. 1, 2010, pp. 251–284.

Zapf, Dieter, Carmen Knorz, and Matthias Kulla, "On the Relationship Between Mobbing Factors, and Job Content, Social Work Environment, and Health Outcomes," *European Journal of Work and Organizational Psychology*, Vol. 5, No. 2, 1996, pp. 215–237.